Loving My Abuser
Through the eyes of the 7th child

By: Mike Antheny

Copyright © 2013 Mike Antheny

All rights reserved.

ISBN: 0991230418

ISBN-13: 978-0-09912304-1-9

DEDICATION

There's no way I could dedicate this book to only one person. So many wonderful people have had an instrumental role in so many ways. I would like to first thank my beautiful mother. Mama, you are a strong and loving woman and without you there's no me. Never has my love for you ever wavered.

Thanks to my wonderful children. Vernon, Artice, Kamiya and Mykail. Parenting was not as hard as it was suppose to be. I am sure each of you was the reason for that. To be a good father was what I strived for and even though I am sure I fell short in some areas, I never fell short in my love for each one of you. I will always love you.

To my amazing sisters and brothers, we have gone through so much together. The odds were against us since birth. What we've been through was not easy but I'm glad it was all of you that I had to go through this with.

† Rest In Peace †

A special thank you to my brother Carl. You have always been someone I admired and a role model to follow. Thank you so much for being there for me in ways that you couldn't imagine. I love you and miss you.

Thanks to the mother of my children, Celestine. Thank you for your unconditional love you had for me. I have no idea why God loaned me one of his Angels but I am forever indebted. I hope that I made good on my last promise and words to you. I love you always.

Mike Antheny

Table of Contents

DEDICATION III
ACKNOWLEDGMENTS VIII
REFLECTION 1
THIS OLD HOUSE 3
PARENTS 5
ABLAZE 8
THE GHOST 14
GRANNY'S HOUSE 17
NEW HOME 23
1ST GRADE 29
THE ART 33
GOODBYE CEDRIC 44
RULE # 100 52
MAN DOWN 60
ANGER MANAGEMENT 62
ON THE ROCKS 65
SPLIT PERSONALITY 68
THE PROMISE 74
FLASHLIGHT 79
THE GOOD SEED 84
MY SAVIOR 88

ALL SCREWED UP	91
SOUL PAIN LINE	104
MATERIALISTIC	111
NEW SCHOOL	114
THE BIG FIGHT	118
ACTING OUT	125
EASTER SPECIAL	128
THE BREAK	134
AFTER SCHOOL SPECIAL	139
GOOD GLIMPSE	150
ENVY	153
THOUGHTLESS	158
TENNIS ANYONE	169
THE LAST STRAW	173
FREE TO ROAM	182
SOUTHERN COMFORT	196
HOME SWEET HOME	203
ABOUT THE AUTHOR	213

ACKNOWLEDGMENTS

Acknowledgement has to be given to those who saw me through this book; to all those who provided support, advised, read, critiqued, offered comments and assisted in the editing and proofreading. I thank you from the bottom of my heart.

Letitia Collins & Monique Forest, I want to thank each of you for taking time out of your lives to help me in many of the ways I have listed above. I am so grateful for your patience, intelligence, and dedication to seeing this through. Thank you both for all your support.

REFLECTION

Ideally when people reflect on their childhood memories, they reflect on happy times, innocent moments and warm and fuzzy feelings. Unfortunately, the reality of my upbringing takes me to a place of overwhelming sadness, darkness and unspeakable rage.

When I think back on my childhood memories, I feel nothing but regret and pain. My memory of those days depresses me to the point of feeling as if I want to cry. For many years, I ignored my feelings. It was my thought that boys and men were not supposed to show their emotions. I thought that showing my emotions would be a sign of weakness. I was told that men were not supposed to have emotional issues. We were supposed to be strong both physically and mentally.

So I ignored my turbulent memories and tried to forget the turmoil that stewed inside of me. However, I would always find myself face to face with the demons inside of me. I realized that there was no disguising this and the mask was going to have to come off sooner or later.

If I were going to fix this, I knew I could no longer suppress it. I had to face reality and realize that something was wrong. I knew I wasn't going to be mentally prepared to deal with the emotions I sought out to find. I also knew by keeping things inside it would continue to form the monster that was evolving inside of me.

I had so many questions about my life. I knew I couldn't ask my father and as for my mother I just couldn't rehash those monstrous moments. She had gone through so much already. This was going to take a lot of courage, a lot of crying, and a lot of healing.

THIS OLD HOUSE

Most kids around the age of 5 years old can only remember bits and pieces of their childhood. It's always a great feeling to be able to reminisce about the good and exciting things that happened in your life. Unfortunately, my childhood memories were filled with horrific events. There were some happy times sprinkled in there now and then, but the bad times outweighed the good.

I was born in Los Angeles, California on November 15, 1964. I was the seventh child born to my parents Jack and Marla Thompson. At the time I was born my family and I lived in South Los Angeles on 36th and Broadway. It is about ten minutes from the downtown area.

The neighborhood was located in an area that was predominantly black. In that area, all the houses were pretty much the same. They had huge front porches, pointed rooftops, faded paint and yellowish colored grass mixed with dirt. Summers back then were mostly hot.

Temperatures were often in the 90's and the heat waves would last for long stretches at a time. I doubt the houses back then had air conditioners in them, but every house did have a basement. I thought it was a cool touch. Our house was a single story home, about 1,100 square feet with 3 bedrooms, 2 baths and a basement. In this particular part of the area, homes were huge but ours was considered a small home.

Most two-story homes looked like haunted houses. We didn't have much in our home, but we did have the basics. We had a gold sofa, love seat and a floor-model T.V. My parents slept in the front bedroom with my younger sister Sharon, who was about 3 years old. They didn't waste any money on a crib. She had been sleeping with them since she came home from the hospital.

My sisters Rhonda, Tonya, Cathy and Diane slept in the middle bedroom. They all had twin beds. I have no idea how my father was able to squeeze four beds into a ten by ten room, not to mention a couple of dressers. My brothers and I slept in the bedroom that was located way in the back of the house.

I shared a twin bed with my brother Gerald. My oldest brother Cedric had his own twin bed. Of course, as kids you don't think that the living arrangements are over-crowded but looking back I realized my parents made do with what they had.

PARENTS

My mom was born in Lake Cormorant, Mississippi and was raised by both her parents who had a total of twelve children. So being in a large family was nothing new to my mother.

My mother stood about five feet, four inches with a medium build. Her skin was a light brown complexion. She had high cheekbones that made her smile even when she wasn't. She had thick, black, silky hair that went a little past her shoulders. She would often hot comb her hair and add curls that made it look even nicer. She was also a conservative dresser. My mom wore pants mostly and only on special occasions would she wear a dress or a skirt.

I always thought my mother was a beautiful woman. She was more of an introvert and always kept to herself when she was around other adults. Rarely did I hear my mom argue. She was soft-spoken, kind, loving and just a sweet woman. She definitely fits the "southern woman" profile.

She had a great personality that was out of this world and a beautiful smile. Now my father, on the other hand, was very unique in many ways. He stood about five feet eleven inches, average weight, with a nice muscular build. He had the kind of build that appeared as if he had worked out at some point in his life, yet his physique was natural. My father's complexion was dark. He wore a thick mustache and a thin beard. He often changed his hairstyle from a short-cropped style to a medium sized Afro.

He was a very stylish man and everything he wore had to be coordinated. He always made sure my mom pressed his clothes perfectly, as his appearance was very important to him. My father loved wearing cologne and rarely did he go a day without it.

His favorite cologne was Brut 33, which I remember so well and will know that smell for the rest of my life. Brut 33 had a fresh out of the shower smell. I have to admit it was a nice scent. My father had a personality that commanded attention. He had a cocky demeanor about himself that you could definitely notice right away. I don't think it was intentional at all, I think it was just apart of who he was.

I've viewed a lot of photos that my father was in and he would have that same self-assuring look. He often stood tall with confidence bigger than life itself. He was a charming individual. When he smiled, you could see that one of his front teeth were outlined in gold.

I guess that is how they did things back in the south where he was from. I can see why my mother fell in love with him. I also can see why family and friends gravitated towards him. He was smooth and charismatic, an attraction that often made people like him. This was the side of my father I admired and that I wanted to be like. Everyone would say to me, "Boy you look just like your father" and I would smile and stand proudly.

Why not? Everyone seemed to really like my father and what young boy wouldn't want to be just like his dad? My father was originally from Glenmora, Louisiana and his parents had a total of seven children. They had four girls and three boys. His mom packed up his four sisters and moved to California after her marriage to his father failed. She left my father and his two brothers to be raised by my grandfather.

According to a few close family members, my grandfather allegedly beat my father. I was told that my grandpa was mean, strict and never whipped his children with a belt but used an extension cord instead.

Eventually, my father ran away from home at the age of fifteen literally traveling as a hobo with a stick. He hopped from train to train until he later ended up in Los Angeles, California where he met my mother and ultimately married her.

ABLAZE

There was nothing to do around the house. I was not in school, I didn't have any friends and Gerald was at school most of the time. I found myself playing with shoes pretending they were cars or army men.

The front porch was basically my playground and I remember playing there often. Mainly because that was the furthest my father would allow me to go. Occasionally, I was allowed to roam the front yard but that was only if my mom or siblings were out there. Our front porch was about 8 feet by 6 feet. That seemed huge to me as a child.

I remember my first time getting in trouble. There was this old rickety chair that sat on our porch. It was light brown with a paisley print. It was wide and it had a high back almost like a king's throne. On this particular day, I was bored and looking for things to do. I noticed that the chair had some type of stringy material hanging down from the bottom.

It was actually wool that they used along with cotton to fill the chair. I had nothing else to do and I thought it would be helpful if I tried to fix the chair by removing the strings. I got on my knees and pulled on the string. As I pulled one string, more string would hang down. After pulling out what seemed to be a handful of strings, to no avail, I knew I would have to find another method. I got off my knees and went inside the house to see if I could find some scissors, a knife or something.

When I went inside the house, I heard my mother in the kitchen preparing dinner. The sound of pots and pans was clanging and whatever mom was cooking smelled good. I knew I couldn't go inside the kitchen to get a knife, so I just began to look around the living room for something that I could use.

I noticed a lighter on the coffee table where my father normally sat and smoked his cigarettes. I had never used a lighter before, but I always saw how my father flicked the lighter to light his cigarettes. I thought I could use a lighter to quickly burn the strings off the bottom of the chair.

This would be perfect I thought to myself. I grabbed a lighter and went back outside. I got on my knees, reached under the chair and flicked the lighter. All I saw was a spark. I flicked the lighter again and again but still nothing but sparks.

I started to think maybe the lighter didn't work but I gave it one more try and finally the lighter lit.

A devilish smile came across my face as my plan went forward. I decided to start with the longest string first. What I didn't know was that piece of string would light up like a fuse to a bomb.

When I lit one piece of string, it quickly spread to the other pieces of strings. Before I knew it, the whole chair was engulfed in flames.

I jumped out of the way in the nick of time to prevent the flames from catching on to me as well. For a few seconds, I watched in horror. I was petrified and my heart was racing. After the initial shock had worn off, it seemed as if the world was in slow motion and the fire was in warp speed. My head turned from side to side looking for help, but there was no one nearby.

I couldn't believe it! I was only trying to burn a few strings. I looked around again for help, an adult or kid but again there was no one. I was terrified with no clue what to do.

All of a sudden my instinct took over and I dropped the lighter and ran into the house for dear life. Part of me wanted to tell my mother what I had done, but I was so afraid of getting in trouble that I ran to my room instead.

I closed the door and stood there shaking, frightened and my heart pounding. I suspected that the chair was fully engulfed by now, but I wasn't going back to see. I had to keep this to myself no matter how hard it would be. Should I act as if I was innocent or should I tell my mother so the house would not burn down?

The only plan that I could think of was to stay in my room and pretend I was just as shocked as anyone else.

Suddenly, there was a knock at the front door and then the doorbell rang. Out of curiosity I hurried out of my room and stopped in the hallway to see who it was.

My mother answered the door and all she could see was clouds of white smoke coming from a soaking wet and charred chair. It was a neighbor from across the street. The neighbor told my mother that he saw the fire when he opened his front door and he ran to our house to put the fire out.

He also told my mother that earlier he had seen me on the porch playing. I was glad that the neighbor saw the fire and rushed to put it out, but I was not happy to hear that he actually saw me on the porch. Apparently the fire wasn't as big as I thought it was but to a five year old I thought I set the whole house ablaze.

There I was standing in the living room with my heart beating so hard I could feel it without touching my chest. My mom turned to me with a look of frustration and asked me if I had started the fire. I knew I was already busted and so I didn't want to make matters worse so I admitted it and said yes. My mom was furious.

The neighbor told my mom he found a lighter nearby on the ground as he handed the lighter to her. My mother graciously thanked the neighbor and closed the door. She then turned to me with an expression I rarely saw.

Her anger definitely showed as she yelled at me and asked me where I got a lighter. Nervously, I told her it was on the coffee table where daddy smoked. She then asked me why I set the chair on fire.

I told her I didn't mean to and that I was just trying to fix the strings that were hanging from the bottom of the chair. She told me to never, ever touch a lighter again and to go to my room. She told me she would tell my father what I did when he got home from work and let him handle me.

My mother was the type that would verbally chastise you and threaten to whip you if you did something wrong, but she would rarely follow through. I guess she assumed that it made no sense in whipping us twice because whether she whipped us or not my father was going to whip us anyway.

Whenever my mom could, she would hide things that we did wrong just to save us from beatings that she knew my father would give us. She would only tell my father if she knew for a fact that he would find out. Unfortunately, in this situation her hands were tied, as he would want to know why his old chair was still smoldering.

As expected, when my father got home I could hear my mom telling him what happened. Without hesitation, my father came straight to my room with a belt in his hand. He didn't ask me anything. All he did was utter a few expletives as he began to whip me. My father whipped me for a few minutes swinging downward as hard as he could.

I cried and told him I was sorry and that I didn't mean to start a fire. My father really laid into me that evening. Either that was my first whipping or just the first one that I remember.

Somehow I felt I deserved that whipping. After all, I could have burned the whole house down. After my father had whipped me, he told me that I had to stay in my room until he said I could come out. He told me I could only come out to eat and use the restroom. When it came to my father a simple beating never sufficed. He would often add on some type of punishment.

If my memory serves me right, I was on a punishment for about a week but in children's time it felt like a month. I had to stay in my room from sun up to sun down. I was only allowed to eat, use the restroom or to take a bath.

The tenderness on my bottom lasted a long time to serve as a reminder way past the length of my punishment. After that incident, I never touched a lighter or matches from that point on. As for the chair, it was thrown away and never replaced.

THE GHOST

It's no surprise that my parents practically emulated their parents by having eight children of their own. They are from the south where big families were normal. I am the second to the youngest of eight children. That makes me the seventh born.

My siblings were born in steps each being around two years apart. From the oldest to the youngest were Cedric, Cathy, Tonya, Rhonda, Diane, Gerald, Sharon and myself. We all got along well and we were pretty close. I guess living in close quarters and not going outside very often will do that.

We ate, slept, laughed and cried together. The boys didn't socialize much with the girls for some odd reason. I don't know if this was strategically done by my father or if it was just happenstance. Many of us believed it was my father's doing because my father controlled everything that happened in our family.

We basically hung out in our rooms. The room that my brothers and I shared wasn't big at all.

I believe the size of the room was eight feet by eight feet. Cedric being older than us had the luxury of his own bed while Gerald and I shared a twin bed sleeping at opposite ends. Gerald was older than I was by two years. He had a very thin build that made it easier to share a bed with him. Cedric's bed was on the opposite wall from ours. We only had one window in our room and that was above Cedric's bed. The window was abnormally high for a bedroom so there was no looking out of our window.

We didn't have much in our room besides two beds, a shared dresser and four walls. However it was our sanctuary and we learned to love it. On some late nights when Gerald and I were supposed to be going to sleep we would often play. It was really the only unsupervised time we could have fun. We were cautious to not let our parents hear us so we were very quiet. One of the other reasons we kept quiet was because Cedric was serious about his sleep and would shush us when we were getting too loud for him.

Gerald and I were sitting on the bed playing while the lights were off. Suddenly we both saw something that startled us and we immediately froze. It appeared to be a glowing, ghostly figure hovering on the wall above our bed.

Our smiles instantly turned upside down as we stared at what we thought was a ghost. We continued to look at the wall in fear as we were literally frozen. At the same time, we looked at each other and I could tell my brother was frightened to death.

If I looked anything like he did then he knew, I was frightened, as well. Without uttering a word, we both jumped from our bed to Cedric's bed without touching the floor.

Our actions startled Cedric and he woke up and yelled, "What is wrong with y'all?" Frantically we told him we saw a ghost on the wall. He said there's no such thing as ghosts. He told us to go back to our bed. We tried to convince him that what we saw on the wall was a ghost.

We begged and pleaded for him to allow us to sleep with him. He hesitated and looked directly at me and said, "Oh no, you are not going to pee in my bed." I was a bed wetter and he knew if he allowed me to sleep in his bed I would wet it. I continued to cry and beg and I guess it eventually got to him because he gave in and said, "ok." Either that or he was too tired to go back and forth.

So we all slept crammed on Cedric's twin bed. Gerald and I both slept at the foot of the bed with the blankets over our heads the entire night. The next morning we all woke up checking ourselves for wetness. The ghost on the wall must have scared the piss out of me because we were all dry.

In hindsight, I don't think it was a ghost at all. I think it was some type of light or reflection from outside that was shining through a tree and then through our window. Regardless of what it was, that night was the beginning of me sleeping with my head under the cover and the last time Gerald and I stayed up to play.

GRANNY'S HOUSE

My sisters pretty much hung around each other for the most part. They all stayed in their room doing whatever they could to entertain themselves. They didn't whine about not having toys, friends or not being able to go outside. In fact, we all had gotten so use to being in the house it no longer bothered us. It just became second nature.

My sisters got along well with each other. There was no bickering of any kind. Not even disputes. They weren't allowed to date or hang out so the times they spent together made them very close. Occasionally my siblings were allowed to go down the street to our cousin's house.

My cousins were around the same age as my older sisters and brothers. Needless to say, my sisters enjoyed getting out of the house and going there to visit. The other times we all were allowed to get out of the house were when we visited my father's mother. She only lived around the corner from us and we would walk to her house.

That was something we as a family did often. Going to my grandmother's house was not that bad to me although some of my older siblings didn't care too much for going there. I actually liked it because there was nothing to do at home. Also for some reason my father never argued while we were there and that was always welcomed.

My father appeared to be very close to his mother. Whenever he was around her, he had a sense of calmness. Something I never saw when he was at home. I don't know if he was acting or if this was the side of him that only his mother could bring out. My siblings said they didn't like going to my grandmother's house that much because she was mean and strict just like my father.

They were much older than I was so maybe she was and I just didn't know better but she really didn't seem that way to me. She definitely was no push over, but I thought she was very sweet. She was quiet, had a dark complexion and she was heavyset. She always wore prescription glasses that were shaped like cat eyes.

As for my paternal grandfather I couldn't personally tell you much about him. I was told he and my father's personality was so much alike. I don't remember ever meeting my dad's father but if my father were like his father, I could only imagine what my dad had to go through as a child. As I saw more and began to understand the kind of strong personalities my grandparents had, it became clear to me why my father had a dominant personality.

My grandmother had a nice size house with a large front porch. It was much bigger than ours. Her house had two levels and was huge.

She kept it neat and tidy and there was nothing out of place.

She had these fancy lamps with tassels hanging from the laminated lampshades. Her couch, chair and love seat were all covered in plastic. Summer time was the worst time to sit on my grandmother's furniture because I would start sweating from the moment I sat down.

I decided whenever I went to her house I was either going to sit on the floor or stand. In the walkways of my grandmother's house were plastic runners covering the floor. You can tell she was not used to having children around. I remember a funny moment about my grandmother. Whenever there were any fast movements or loud noises around her, it would drive her nuts. She'd get agitated and say, "All right now, y'all need to go outside with that." She did not say that in a pleasant voice either and we knew it was time to go outside.

Every Sunday, my family and grandmother, would go to the church that was just up the street. We didn't have to drive, but my father drove anyway.

Initially, I did not understand what church was about. It was never explained to me in any kind of way. All I knew a man would stand in front of everyone, sweating, yelling and reading from this book they called the Bible.

There were a lot of well-dressed people there focused and listening to his every word while silently holding their bible.

They seemed to understand what he was saying but because I didn't understand any of it, I quickly became bored and I found myself fighting to stay awake. Church was definitely too long for a child who didn't understand it.

Many times I tried to stay awake and act as if I was interested, but my eyelids became so heavy and my head began to bob back and forth. This was a constant struggle throughout the sermon. Whenever I woke up I would look towards my parents to see if they saw me but they were looking straight ahead. I was trying everything I could think of to stay awake. I took deep breaths; changed positions and I even tried to look around the church at other things that might keep my attention.

I noticed that I wasn't the only kid in church fighting to stay awake. Half of the kids in there looked like zombies with their eyes half open. They would look at me and I would look at them and it was a language unspoken. I knew exactly how they felt.

The only thing that gave life into the church and grabbed my attention was when the choir began to sing. The choir gave the church that lift of energy opposite from that mundane feeling you got from the pastor's sermon. People were either clapping, singing or some were standing. It was a totally different vibe that instantly cured my boredom.

If only the choir could perform more often I could stay awake and figure this church thing out. I did have a frightening experience one Sunday while I was in church. The pastor was in one of his deep sermons and he was preaching from the top of his lungs.

He paced back and forth on the stage and the congregation was yelling, "Thank you, Jesus." The guy playing the organ would mash down on the organ keys in order to hype up the moment. Everyone was engaged and some of them stood up and told the preacher to preach.

There was this older lady in particular, she was thin, 65 years old and she wore a dark dress and a large hat with flowers around it. She stood up, walked to the middle of the isle and she began dancing right where she stood.

She was moving her feet as if she was running in place but in slow motion. She began turning around and around very slowly while yelling, "Hallelujah" and "Thank you Jesus." Then she stopped, looked towards the ceiling, raised her hands up high and began shaking as she fell to the floor.

Some of the church members ran to her aid and started fanning her with those paper fans that they leave in the back of the pews. I remember thinking why isn't anyone calling the ambulance? No one panicked or anything. Suddenly across the room another person fell out and then another. Now this was when I really began to get scared.

I didn't know what was attacking everyone, but I thought it would be best for all of my family to leave. My parents didn't seem to be affected by what was going on because they didn't budge. All I could do was hope that whatever was happening didn't get back to where we were. Everyone began clapping including my parents.

I wondered why they were all so happy? What's going on? It wasn't until after the next few Sundays that I found out that people were catching the holy ghosts. I noticed that this was common and natural amongst churchgoers.

I still didn't understand it, but I learned to anticipate it. There was only one thing I really liked about going to church and that was getting an ice cream cone after the services were over.

After the service, the church gave out ice cream cones to whoever wanted one. That was the only time I thought church wasn't so bad. Well, at least until next Sunday came again.

NEW HOME

In early 1971, our family moved to a new house on 130th Street and Avalon Blvd. Although this area bordered the cities of Compton, L.A. and Gardena we were considered to live in Los Angeles. I was 6 years old when we moved there. It was a great upgrade from our old house.

It was brand new and no one had lived in it before us. It was a 4 bedroom, 1 ¼ bath and about 1,200 square feet. The house had an attached garage located in front of the house. When you entered the house, you were immediately in the living room and to the right were the kitchen and dining room.

The house had a long hallway that ran right up the middle of the bedrooms and bathrooms. The hallway seemed to go on forever. My parent's bedroom was located in the far back of the house on the right side and the boys' bedroom was located just across form theirs. The girls had the front two bedrooms that were on the same side as the boys bedroom, but closer to the front of the house. I really liked the house.

It had a nice modern style to it and totally different from our old home. The house sat on a steep incline with no concrete anywhere.

In fact, everything around the house was dirt. The street and sidewalk were not paved at the time.

There were new houses on both sides of us that were not yet occupied and the neighborhood appeared to be very quiet and vacant. I remember my brothers and I had to watch our new house to prevent the house from being vandalized while my parents were bringing items from our old house to our new house.

I was scared that we had to be in the new house without my parents. It was just my brothers and I and having my brothers there was no security blanket for me. I think they were just as scared as I was.

My parents went back and forth during the day bringing items from the old house. When it got too late, they stayed at our old house with the girls. Thank God it was only for a couple of days. Besides being scared, I was getting tired of eating cold cereal for breakfast and sandwiches for dinner.

Finally, we had moved out of our old house and into our new home. My father was determined to make it the best house on the block.

My father was the type that could make five dollars an hour seem like he was making fifty dollars an hour. He lived as if he was rich and above anyone else.

Of course, he was not rich but because he did the work himself, he could afford to buy nicer things. His plan was to have everything paved around the house. He was definitely a do-it-yourself type of guy. Of course, this is not without the help of his children who to him were free laborers. Sometimes my father would ask my uncles and their sons to help.

I remember one project in particular where my father asked my cousin Frank to help us. Frank was around the same age as Cedric. They were very close and hung around each other a lot. At 6 years old, normally I would be considered young but with my father age was not a reason for not being able to work.

In his eyes if you could walk you could work. At the supervision and yelling of my father, my job was to fetch the tools that were needed. The work seemed like it was non-stop.

I was ripping and running to get tools and half the time I didn't even know what they were. Luckily, Gerald was with me and together we were able to get the things my father wanted. We didn't get a break or have breakfast or anything. We worked relentlessly. It was a hot and busy day.

The temperature was in the 80's and we had been out there since seven o'clock that morning.

There was no laughter or anything just hard work and sweat. It might not have been so bad had my father not screamed at us at every task he had us do.

He was rushing us to get it done quickly because he had ordered a cement truck to pour the cement and the truck was on the way. Knowing my father if he was able to pour the cement himself, he would have. My father got a posthole digger and dug a hole 4 feet deep. Then Cedric, Frank and my father picked up a long wooden pole that was about 14 feet high and placed it into the hole. Gerald and I looked at each other and we had a little smirk on our face. To our surprise we realized that our father was building a basketball court for us to play on.

Soon after placing the pole in the hole the cement truck arrived. The cement was poured and all the cement was laid around the house completing our job.

My father asked Cedric and my cousin Frank if they wanted to carve their names into the concrete on the side of the house. They said," Yes" and they each took turns carving their first names into the wet cement. Unfortunately, Gerald and I weren't asked even though we were working our tails off just like them. I don't know about Gerald, but I felt unappreciated. I'm not sure if we weren't asked because we were too young, but it definitely wasn't a good feeling.

A couple of days later after the cement had dried my father installed a backboard to the long pole he had placed into the ground. This was exciting to me because it was something my brothers and I could enjoy together. The disappointment of not being able to carve my name in the cement the other day quickly dissipated.

While working that day, I had a little pep in my step. If I knew how to whistle, I would have done it while I was working. I was so excited. For some reason, time didn't go by fast enough but I didn't mind. If my father yelled at me that day, I didn't even notice it.

Nothing could have upset me that day. I was waiting for my father to let us know when we could play on the basketball goal. Instead, we were told never to play on it. In fact, he never purchased a basketball. I guess the basketball goal was there for show. I had no clue why he wouldn't let us play basketball back there other than the fact that we were always on punishment. I was devastated. I went to my room and cried.

The very next week it was time to build a fence around our property. My father decided to use wood planks around the backyard and cinder blocks for the side of the house leading to the front. The wood planks were six feet tall by six inches wide.

During the time we were building a fence around our property my father woke us up at seven in the morning every weekend. We worked from sun up to sun down. It didn't matter if it was cold or hot. We only stopped to eat lunch and dinner.

I am not sure how long it took to do the entire gate around the house, but it seemed like an eternity for a 6 year old kid. When the fence was finally done, it was nice. The gate in front of the driveway was designed with a wooden gate that would swing outward to allow my father's car to get in and out of the driveway.

We didn't have to swing the entire gate to enter the yard because he built a small gate for people to walk through.

It was definitely different from the normal chain link gates that the rest of the neighborhood had.

I learned how to use all kinds of tools, lay cement and build a fence at the tender age of 6 years old. My father was creative when it came to building things and that was something I really liked about him.

1ST GRADE

I began first grade later that year in September of 1971. I was 6 years old. I didn't know my alphabets or numbers, but I could identify just about every tool in my father's toolbox. School was new to me because I didn't attend pre-school or kindergarten. I didn't quite get the concept of school, but I was anxious to see what it was all about. My days of staying in the house while all my other siblings were able to leave and get a well deserved break from home was over.

Although Gerald had been in school where we use to live, this was his first time at this particular school. The school we were attending was called Mark Twain Elementary. It was less than a mile from our house, three minutes in the car and a fifteen-minute walk. My father thought the school was close enough to walk. So Gerald and I did just that.

My siblings were all in school, as well. Some were in high school and some were in junior high. They went to schools a bit further than mine yet some of my older siblings had to walk.

The ones that went to a school that was much further were able to use public transportation. I didn't mind the idea of walking to school. I thought it would be fun and a chance to play. The route we took was simple and pretty much straightforward. We had to cross Avalon Boulevard and then walked through a huge vacant field. After the field, there was a short street we walked down that led directly to the front gates of Mark Twain Elementary School.

Across from the school was a huge water tank. It must have been a thousand feet high and supplied water to the nearby residents and school. Once Gerald and I got to school we had to part ways and go to our classroom that was labeled on a piece of paper that our mom had given us before we left. As I was walking to find my classroom, I saw a lot of children just as lost as I was. It was a good thing there were a few teachers in the hallway to point us in the right direction.

I finally approached my classroom and I opened the door. A beautiful woman welcomed me inside and asked to see my paperwork. I showed it to her and she introduced herself as Mrs. Taylor, the teacher for this class. She showed me where to sit and she began instructing the class. I was nervous, but I gradually adjusted.

The setting was different. I was around other children my age and I was able to be a kid. We read a lot in Mrs. Taylor's class that day. That was fine by me because it was my favorite past time and something I did almost every day at home.

At home, I often lost track of time while reading. No matter what I was reading I imagined being wherever the story took place.

Reading definitely helped me. I was having so much fun in Mrs. Taylor's class. Before I knew, it was time to close our books and get ready to go home. The first day of school was pretty much a success and I couldn't wait for tomorrow. I enjoyed being at school more than I did at home.

My teacher was very nice and beautiful too may I add. I took an instant liking to her and I wanted to impress her by being a great student. She was definitely one of the reasons I enjoyed her class. She always had a smile on her face and her voice was pleasantly soft and soothing. She always taught with a smile and never once raised her voice. I could tell she really enjoyed teaching.

The other reason I liked Mrs. Taylor's class was because of my new friend David. David was dark skinned, a few inches shorter than I was and chubby. He was a cool kid and he was very playful. David and I didn't talk in the classroom, as Mrs. Taylor was not having that. We actually met on the playground and hit it off. We later found out that he and I lived around the corner from each other. I still didn't get to play with him because of my father's restrictions.

Whenever David came over to see if I could come out to play my father would say no. So we would make up for that time while on the school playground.

My mother at that time began working for the Mattel Toy Company. She would always bring my brother and I some toy cars to play with.

I remember the round car holder that was shaped like a wheel. It was full of cars. I think that was my first real toy or just the toy I treasured the most.

My father was the primary breadwinner in my family earning good money as a local truck driver.

He worked over ten hours a day and would come home tired and ready to eat. Although my mom worked as well, she would get off a few hours before my father and prepare the food for the family. My mother's work was never done it seemed.

She often came home from work around two o'clock in the afternoon and began working all over again.

She would cook dinner, clean the house, make sure all the children were doing what they were supposed to be doing and then she made sure my father's plate was ready when he came home from work.

Having the house settled before my father came home was not a huge task for my mother. She had so much experience that she was able to do this with her eyes closed.

My father had a specific way he wanted his house ran and it was going to be ran his way or no way.

THE ART

When my father came home from work he would open the door, walk to the couch and throw his keys on the coffee table. He would then take the items out of his pockets and place them all on the table. He then would unbuckle his pants, sit down, take off his work boots and watch T.V. At that point my mother knew it was time to bring him his plate. This was my father's routine every Monday through Friday around five or six o'clock each evening.

There was an art to a lot of things when dealing with my father for instance how his food had to be prepared on his plate. For instance you were not to put his breads next to anything that had juice running from it like cabbage, greens, etc. My mother knew exactly how to prepare my father's plate.

I can only imagine the hard knocks it took for her to get to that point. Especially if it was anything like the hard knocks my sisters were going through. With my father, if you didn't get it right the first time you were going to feel it one way or another.

There was no learning curve with him. He took time to teach each one of my sisters how to cook except for Sharon because she was too young at the time. Even if you didn't want to learn how to cook you had no say in the matter anyway. None of my sisters wanted to learn how to cook especially with my father as their instructor.

I remember one Saturday morning my father woke all my sisters up at about five in the morning to make breakfast. Now I am not talking about just a bowl of cereal, I am talking about a breakfast fit for a king. He had them make scrambled eggs, bacon, sausages, grits, rice, pancakes and biscuits. He showed them how to cut up pineapple, watermelon and cantaloupes in a certain way.

He also taught them how to arrange the fruit for centerpieces for the table. My father had my sisters prepare breakfast not only for our immediate family but also for our relatives who knew about this big breakfast every Saturday morning. Everything had to be made a certain way and the table had to be set perfectly. The knives, forks and spoons, were all on top of the perfectly folded napkins.

I had to admit that the end result was beautiful, but the road to getting to that point was very hard on my sisters. While my sisters were preparing breakfast, I heard him yelling and screaming at them constantly. In between the yelling I heard slaps and short cries. On occasion dishes and pots were not only being slung around but they were also being thrown.

I knew my sisters were a nervous wreck knowing my father was watching their every move and any wrong move would set him off. While my sisters were making breakfast under the tutelage of my irate father, he made sure to make his way to our room to wake my brother and I to do the yard work. He didn't know that with all the yelling, cursing and screaming he was doing we were up long before he thought about waking us. We often would lie in our beds looking up at the ceiling.

I had so many things going through my head and such a heavy heart for what my sisters and mom were going through. My father yelled for us to get up to do our yard work. We got out of our beds and got dressed. We walked down the hall and through the kitchen straight to the back door. I'd always look down and not at my father or anywhere towards his direction. I knew he was mad and I did not want him to let his frustration out on me.

Gerald and I had to mow the grass, pick up any trash and pick the weeds out of the flowerbeds. We knew to continue to work until we were called in for breakfast. When it came to my father, there was an art to cleaning the yard. The first time I learned about this particular art to cleaning the yard I was dumbfounded.

The backyard had a 10x10 slab of concrete butted up against the back of the house and around the slab of concrete was dirt. Sometimes weeds grew out of the dirt so we had to remove the weeds we saw either with a shovel, hoe or by hand.

After we pulled the weeds and picked up the trash, we thought we were done. We actually finished before my father had a chance to call us in for breakfast so we thought we were doing great time-wise. Normally, whenever we finished the yard, we would roam the yard and pretend we were still working just to be out of his way. This time, so much time had passed before he called us in that we decided to let him know we were done a little earlier.

My brother and I always had this unspoken game where we would find a way to get behind the other when it was time to tell my father something. We did that because we knew the person in front always had to speak first and in some cases duck first. I was the first person this time. So I went inside the house and told him we were finished cleaning the yard. My father said ok and I guess he had to see for himself.

He went out the front door and looked at the front yard. He then walked to the side of the house looking down on the ground as he walked towards the back yard. When he got to the back yard, my father stopped and said, "This backyard is not done, finish it". My father turned around and walked back into the house.

My brother and I looked at each other with puzzled looks on our faces. Without uttering a word to each other, we walked around the backyard aimlessly not knowing what my father saw that was wrong. We decided we were going to redo everything we did before to make sure we didn't overlook anything.

We began to pick up trash we assumed he saw. After double-checking the grounds for another 20 minutes, we went back into the house again to tell my father we were done. This time I made sure Gerald was in front. Sometimes we had to find a reason to be behind the other person.

This time I pretended to see trash on the ground and I reached down to pick it up. This move put Gerald ahead of me. Now Gerald was in front as we went inside the house. Gerald told my father we were done in the backyard.

My father walked out to the backyard again and looked around. Angrily he said, "Look! This yard is not finished. Do not come in that fucking house again until this yard is clean or I am whipping y'all asses". He left and this time we stood there in disbelief. We couldn't believe it. What was it we were missing? Clearly we didn't see anything that he could have possibly seen. At this point, I was scared. Instead of telling us what he felt needed to be cleaned he left it to us to figure it out. Again we picked up anything that we thought my father had seen.

There was nothing else to do. We swept the concrete for the third time. We were on the ground looking like crack heads. Sweat dripping from our brows and locking in on anything white. A thought came to my head that we would be all day picking up every white speck in the dirt. So I grabbed one of those metal flexible rakes and started raking the dirt.

The rake gave us assurance that there were no specks left on the ground. We spent another hour on the yard making sure we didn't miss anything.

We both knew that if we went to get our father this time and the yard was not to his liking we were going to get beat right there on the spot. I am sure breakfast was done a long time ago. Normally my father would have called us in to eat.

It was clear that until we were finished cleaning the backyard we were not going to get in the house to eat. We didn't feel confident, but we knew if we took too long in the backyard it would set him off as well. We were damned if we did and damned if we didn't. So we took that long walk towards the house.

This time I wanted to lead. I don't know if I was delirious from the sun, starving from not eating or if I was getting to the point of not caring. I just wanted to get this over with even if it meant I would get beaten. My father was in the living room sitting on the couch watching T.V. As I walked through the kitchen I could tell everyone had eaten because my sisters were washing dishes.

I walked in the living room and told my father we were done with the backyard. My father hesitated a few seconds, then he got up and walked hastily towards the backyard as if he knew once again we had not finished the yard. Gerald and I walked behind him. My heart was beating fast. As we walked to the backyard with my father, I made sure Gerald was behind him and I was walking behind Gerald.

I was not going to be the first to feel my father's wrath if I could help it. My father looked at the yard. Gerald and I stood nervously behind him at a safe distance. My father turned to Gerald and I and said, "Now it's done and next time this is how I want it done before you tell me you're finished." My father told us to put the tools away and go inside to eat. He then walked back into the house. My father never told us what he was looking for each time he checked out the yard.

Then it dawned on me. The only thing we did differently was raked the dirt. The rake left long lines in the dirt that gave it that farmer's garden look. That is what my father was looking for all that time. It did look neater, but I never understood why he couldn't just tell us what to do. What was that all about?

My father was a very controlling and prideful man and for some reason we were supposed to know what he wanted us to do without him telling us what to do. I guess for him to tell us was too easy. It wasn't right, but this is how he was towards us.

After we put the tools away my brother and I went into the house to eat. I was exhausted. The sun and fear had taken its toll on me. The work was no problem as I could do it while standing on my head. I was just relieved that this ordeal was over. I remember going into the house and seeing the amazing table setting that my sisters had prepared for breakfast. It was huge and the most breakfast food I have ever seen.

I would never have an issue with waking up early to do yard work if I knew a feast like this would be awaiting me. After washing my hands, I rushed to the table. Normally we would all sit at the table as a family but this time we were late from doing the yard work. Even though everyone had already eaten there still was a lot of food left on the table. I didn't know where to start.

I think it was all a blur for me at that point. I ate everything that was in front of me. I am not even sure if my brother was at the table when I started. All I knew was that I was starving. Times to feast like this didn't come often.

During the week, we usually had beans and rice for dinner and grits and oatmeal for breakfast. Rarely did we have lunch or a menu change. The best part of breakfast was that I did not have to eat while my father was at the table. After eating everything on my plate, I started eating the cantaloupes. Then I ate a slice of pineapple, some grapes and watermelon. After stuffing my face, I washed it all down with a tall glass of fresh squeezed orange juice.

You could easily assume I was preparing for hibernation and that wasn't too far from the truth. One thing I have to say is that my father always encouraged us to eat as much as we wanted on Saturday mornings. He didn't have to tell me twice. I was always a hefty eater. Since we were not allowed to go into the refrigerator without his permission, I would eat as much as I could to hold me until the next meal.

When I was finished eating, I went to my room and grabbed a book to read until dinner. Dinnertime was considered an important time for all of us to sit together as one big family. I have no clue why because we were not allowed to talk.

My mother and sisters would prepare the meals and serve the food. We had a large dining room table. It was one of those tables that could be made larger by adding a leaf or shortened by removing it. My father bought a kitchen corner nook that we sat on.

He placed it against the wall and that's mostly where the kids sat. My siblings and I were not allowed to utter a word at the table. Not even to ask someone to pass the salt. No one at the dinner table spoke. We tried the playing and giggling game and it didn't go well and that was the day we learned to just eat.

While at the dining room table, my siblings and I would try to make the other person laugh or giggle. We knew whoever laughed would get in trouble. On this particular evening, we were all eating and it was quiet.

My father and mother were looking down as they ate and you couldn't hear anything other than the clanking of silverware hitting against the plates and the sound of food being chewed.

As I looked around I could see that a few of my siblings were trying to make each other laugh. They were sneaking in funny faces, when my father wasn't looking. My father always ate with his head down and chewed his food like he was in a hurry to eat.

My mom went back and forth from the table to the cabinets getting things my father requested.

As I watched my siblings play their game, I knew something bad was about to happen. Cathy was on the verge of bursting up.

She looked like she could not hold her laugh in any longer. She was actually turning red while trying hard not to laugh. It was like I was watching it in slow motion.

Suddenly Cathy burst out laughing causing the food in her mouth to fly everywhere. The worse part of this was that my father happened to be sitting directly in front of her. The food she held in her mouth went flying right into my father's face and plate. All the laughter ceased instantly.

I knew Cathy was about to get the beating of her lifetime. Cathy's eyes had gotten so large in fear of what she had done. All eyes were on my father. He looked at Cathy and told her to get her fucking ass up from the table.

Cathy quickly got up and went to the room. My father was actually stunned by the look he had on his face. It was weird because we expected him to clear the table with her behind, but he surprised all of us. My mother quickly started cleaning up Cathy's mess.

My father said, "If any of you laugh at this table again I'm going to beat your asses." My mother brought him a fresh plate of food and took his old one. The rest of us continued eating and the laughing game was officially over.

Needless to say, Cathy was done eating for the rest of the night. She was ordered to put the food away and clean the kitchen even though it was not her week.

Cathy had no issue with this order as long as she was still alive. She was also put on punishment. She couldn't eat with us for a month.

Instead, she could only eat after everyone else was done eating. That night was hilarious and frightening at the same time. When I finished eating Gerald and I went to our room where we exploded with laughter. It wasn't Cathy that we were laughing at but that she basically spat in my father's face. To us that was hilarious.

GOODBYE CEDRIC

One of the saddest moments in my life was when my older brother Cedric was going away to the Army. I was 9 years old and in the 4th grade at the time. My siblings and I had always been together and none of us had ever left for a day let alone years. Cedric hadn't been home much anyway because of school and working at McDonald's, but this was different. My older brother was going to the Army for 4 years. I didn't want Cedric to leave. I looked at him as my protector although he was just as scared of pops as I was.

I always hoped one day he would do or say something to stop my father from being so abusive to us. I thought maybe when Cedric got older and bigger than my father he would be able to stand up to him for all of us.

I really had a hard time dealing with the news that Cedric was leaving. None of us actually spoke much to each other in the house and crying was not allowed unless it was at the hands of my father. I didn't know how to deal with my feelings and I didn't have anyone I could go to.

So I had to keep my feelings tucked away with the rest of my emotions. I don't know what lead him to that decision. I assumed my brother just wanted to get out the house and away from my father and I couldn't blame him. If I could have enlisted at my age, I would have. I was at school when Cedric actually left for the Army so I didn't get to say goodbye.

I remember I didn't feel good all day in school. All I could think of was Cedric not being there when I returned. I didn't realize how much I really loved him or how much I was going to miss him until he left. All I could do was hope time would fly and that he would hurry home. My oldest brother leaving home meant Gerald and I would be the only two boys at home.

Gerald was physically no bigger than I was and if anything happened I would end up protecting him before he protected me. Nonetheless, I still had him. I don't know how my father felt about my brother leaving for the Army, but it didn't seem like he was sad about it.

It wasn't a part of my father's character to show emotions unless he was yelling, screaming or disciplining us. As for my mom, she was definitely sad that Cedric left for the Army.

At the same time, I think she was happy too. At least one of her children was away from this crazy man. My mom loved her children and we knew it. Regardless of the situation she would protect us in any way she could.

My mom didn't have any authority in the house. My father ran everything. She wore what he approved, she ate what he approved and she went where he approved. There was nothing in the house that was not approved by my father first.

My mom kept secrets from him as if he was a stranger to save us as well as her. There were times she sneaked us second helpings of food when my father was at work or sleeping. She gave us sandwiches when she knew that my father wouldn't approve. She would even let us have special treats like fruit, ice cream or cookies, but only if she knew my father wouldn't notice that the food was missing. My mother either wasn't allowed to eat what my father ate or she chose not to. I never saw her eat anything other than what her kids ate.

I knew she was an adult, but she basically couldn't do any more than her children could do. It was like he used her as his informant when he wasn't there and his slave when he was. My mom was just as sad, beaten and helpless as we were. One personal issue I had growing up was wetting the bed.

My parent's thought it might have been because I was young and drinking too much water and I didn't know how to get up and use the bathroom. I didn't get in trouble for wetting the bed because my parent's believed it was just a phase and that I would grow out of it. I actually did stop wetting the bed once we moved here to 130th Street.

Now that Cedric was gone Gerald and I no longer had to share the same bed. I think Gerald was happy he and I were no longer sharing a bed because he didn't have to worry about being soaked in the middle of the night. I remember some mornings Gerald would wake up very upset that I peed in the bed. When I wet the bed we would have to get up, change our clothes and sleep on the floor. Sometimes Gerald would find a dry spot on the bed and sleep there. Just when I thought wetting the bed was all behind me it came back.

I remember one day it was about six in the morning and I woke up with my clothes, sheets and mattress soaked from wetting the bed. I got out of bed and turned on the lights. Gerald must have been in a deep sleep because he didn't budge.

I changed my clothes, took the sheet off the bed and threw it up over the top of the curtain, hoping it would dry before morning. I grabbed the blanket that I had on top of me and slept on the floor. It was a lot harder than my bed but at least it was dry. I woke up around 9 o'clock in the morning on my own.

The floor wasn't comfortable at all. I got up and checked the sheet to see if it had dried. It dried a little, but the mattress was still soaked. My mother yelled from the hallway for us to get up. Gerald woke up and noticed the sheet over the window and he knew what had happened the night before. He was all too familiar with this pattern. He opened the window so the room could air out. From the look on his face, he was not happy with how the room smelled.

We got dressed and went outside to do our chores. My mother's daily routine on the weekends was going around the house and collect all the dirty clothes to do her laundry.

Apparently she went to our room and she noticed mine were soiled with urine so she called me into the house. She asked me how often I wet the bed and I told her this was the first time. My mom told me not to drink water after six o'clock at night and to make sure I had used the restroom before I went to bed. She reminded me to let her know if I wet the bed again so she could change my sheet.

I followed my mother's instructions and many mornings were the same. I would wake up wet from peeing in the bed and let her know what had happened. She knew I was using the restroom before I went to sleep and that I was not drinking water after six. Still she didn't understand why I kept wetting the bed.

One morning my father came into our room to wake us up earlier than normal and he noticed a stench in the air. He knew it was pee and he asked me if I had peed in bed. I told him that I did and he asked me how long have I been wetting the bed? I told him that it had been a couple of weeks. My father was furious and asked me if my mother knew about it. I told him yes she knew about it and he darted out the room. My mother was in her bed sleeping.

I could hear him waking her up. He yelled, "Marla, Marla" my mom woke up and said "huh"? He said, "Why in the hell didn't you tell me that Michael was peeing in the bed again?"

My mom said, "Because I thought it would go away". She said, "I told him not to drink water after six and to use the restroom every night before he went to bed". My father was livid. He said, "Were you keeping a secret from me?"

My mom said, "No". He said, "You know damn well I am to know everything that goes on in this mother fucking house".

He told her if she kept something from him again he was going to kick her ass. My father came back into our room and told me if I peed in bed again he was going to beat my ass. Gerald and I were told to grab my mattress and set it outside the front door to dry.

I think he did this to embarrass me because friends and family members would see the mattress outside. He told me to take a bath and then go outside to do my chores. While I was outside doing my chores of course every one that passed by was looking at the mattress. I tried to clean the front yard as fast as I could.

I was embarrassed and upset because I didn't have any control over what I was doing. It's not like I was waking up with the urge to pee and decided to lie there and pee on myself. The next morning my father purposely came into my room to see if I had peed in bed.

He woke me up and told me to get out the bed. I was scared because I knew I had wet the bed again, but I didn't know what he was going to do. As I stood up, my underwear and t-shirt was soaked as well as my sheet. He immediately left the room without saying a word and I stood there practically dripping wet.

He came back into the room with an extension cord and he just started beating the living daylight out of me. He hit me so hard with the extension cord that I could literally feel the whelps burning instantly from the ammonia of my pee.

Each time the extension cord sliced into my skin it would just burn non-stop. I cried and told him I was sorry. I told him I didn't know I was peeing, but he continued to whip me.

He yelled and told me to get up and use the restroom next time. I couldn't help but think how could I do that? Luckily the whipping didn't last long. Just about 20 seconds but I was not keeping time. One second was too long for an accident. After he had whipped me, he told me to take a bath and change my clothes.

He then told me to drag the mattress outside by myself. I was only 9 years old. The mattress clearly outweighed me but again I am sure this was part of his punishment. I couldn't comprehend why I was getting beat for something I had no control over. He didn't even know what to do so how could I? I understood why my mother tried to keep it from him.

She understood it was a mental thing that would go away in time. She helped me as much as she could regardless of the threat he gave her.

When my father was at work in the mornings, my mother would wash my soiled linen. She would find a way to dry my mattress within an hour or two.

I still had my issues peeing in bed and whenever my father found out he never hesitated to beat me for it.

At times, he would combine punishments and beat me a little longer for wetting the bed or for something else I did the night before. I am not sure if I was just a heavy sleeper or the urge to urinate never woke me up?

All I know is that in order to slow it down my mother didn't allow me to have water after three o'clock in the afternoon. She also made me use the restroom before I went to sleep at night and she would wake me up at midnight to use the restroom again. I didn't like getting woke up at midnight every night, but it was better than getting beat every morning.

RULE # 100

My father was an unusually strict man. I'm not saying strict is a bad thing, but even as a child I knew something was wrong. I never had a clue because I was not able to see what went on in other households. So I pretty much thought the treatment was normal.

My father's demeanor was stoic and detached when it came to me. He would never sit down and just talk to me. In fact, the only conversation we had was when he was yelling, cursing and screaming at me. He was not one that I could turn to, learn from, laugh with or look up to. It was a feeling a child should never feel. It was empty and unexplainable. Basically, he was a stranger that had children with my mom. I was afraid of him and I think that is how he wanted it.

If he had any kindness, he was not going to show it to any of his children and especially to me. My father was about rules and he had a lot of them. Breaking one of his rules carried huge consequences.

One rule he had was that every night before we went to bed we had to show him the clothes we were going to wear for school the next morning.

We had to show him our socks, underwear, T-shirt, shirt and pants. Our clothes had to be clean, ironed and all this had to be approved by him. The punishment for not doing so was a beating. If you didn't get your beating right away, it wasn't forgotten just delayed. That sometimes made it even worse because you didn't know when it was coming, but it was coming.

One night I made a mistake and forgot to show my father the clothes I was going to wear to school the next day. I had kitchen duty to do that night and showing my clothes had slipped my mind.

Kitchen duty was a major project in our house. Everyone dreaded this weekly chore. The main reason is that it had to be done a certain way. It seemed as though my father's rules pertaining to washing the dishes were set up for us to fail. Here's an example. I had to make hot dishwater with a large amount of dishwashing liquid, place all of the utensils in the water so they could soak while washing the rest of the dishes. The dishes had to be washed in an exact order.

Glass, plastic, then all pots and pans. If at any time I was washing dishes and the water became dirty or cold, I were to change the water immediately. The last thing that was to be washed was the utensils that had been soaking the whole time.

If my father had caught me washing the dishes in any other order or washing the dishes in dirty or cold water, he then would make me pull every dish out of the cabinets and wash all of them whether they were clean or not.

One day I was up until two o'clock in the morning and this was on a school day.

This is exactly why I forgot to show my father my school clothes. I was tired and sleepy. There was no explaining to him why things didn't get done. He didn't want to hear it and you were liable to get beat on the spot if you tried. On my way out the door to go to school my father informed me that he would be whipping me for not showing him my clothes last night.

I told him ok and went out the door to go to school. I was lucky I didn't get it then. I hated getting whippings before school. It just ruined my whole day. I went through each class at school with the threat my father put on my mind. After school, I was wondering when I was going to get my whipping. I did my homework, ate dinner and even did my chores in the kitchen and still no whipping. This was so hard on me. I was a nervous wreck the whole day.

After doing my chores, I was supposed to show him but he was asleep. Normally my father snored very loud, which definitely was a happy sign. Whenever we heard him snoring we knew he was in a deep sleep.

At other times, he would lay on the couch with one eye on the TV and the other eye on us not snoring at all.

I had a huge dilemma on my hands. I was already in trouble for not showing him my clothes last night and now it's time to show him my clothes again but he is asleep.

I thought if I woke him up to show him my clothes it would be like waking him up to tell him I am ready for my whipping. My choice may not have been a good one, but I just couldn't wake him to beat me.

So I went into the kitchen, turned the lights off and went to my room. I undressed down to my underwear and t-shirt and got into bed. I was so exhausted and was quickly on my way to sleep. Just before I could shut my eyes good enough I heard that infamous sound of his house shoes sliding down the hallway along with the sound of a belt buckle clanging with each slide. My heart began beating and the taste of fear was so thick in my mouth that I couldn't even swallow.

I didn't even breathe because I didn't want the sound of my breathing to drown the sound of his movements. I thought he was asleep. I heard him snoring loudly. All of a sudden I heard a loud bang as my father swung open my door and flicked on the lights. My heart sunk instantly. I was so scared. I took the cover off my head and saw he had a skinny, brown extension cord wrapped tightly around a closed fist. He yelled at me to get up and I scurried out of bed. Right away I knew my decision wasn't good. He asked me why didn't I show him my clothes for school again before I went to bed? I told him because he was asleep and I was going to show him in the morning. I guess that the answer wasn't good enough as my father swung the extension cord at me with all the strength he had.

The impact was enough to paralyze me for half of a second. I couldn't move or breathe. It was like he was using a razor blade as I felt my flesh rip open. While he was beating me, I tried to tell my father that he was asleep when I finished and I didn't want to wake him.

I am sure it didn't come out that way, but I tried. Anything to stop the beating but that fell on deaf ears because my father didn't reply and didn't let up. My father was heavy handed so every swing that came down was intended to do bodily harm.

All I could do was cry, scream and try to soften the blows of the extension cord. He wailed away while I spun around him in circles. It seemed like this painful dance went on for an eternity. He must have enjoyed hearing me cry because if I didn't cry loud enough he would change where he was hitting me to find where it hurt worse. I had to look at him to see if this was really my father? My protector? What I saw frightened me even more.

I could see the grimace on his face, as he would bite his lip and grunt. No compassion, no look as if beating me hurt him more than it hurt me. The look on his face was cold.

I begged and pleaded for him to stop and I told him I was sorry and that I would never do it again. The levels of my screams adjusted with the force of the blows I endured. When he whipped me in the same spot a few times, I screamed for dear life. He had a way to whip the breath out of me.

I wondered if that was his measurement to know he was tearing into me? Well, actually he was tearing deep into my flesh.

When he finished, he told me to get my clothes together and show him my clothes. He left the room and walked back into the living room. I was in so much pain that I could barely walk. As I looked in the drawers for my clothes, my body was just burning all over. I was still crying but at the same time I was trying not to cry loud.

He didn't like when we cried no matter what we were crying for. During the time I was getting beat, Gerald was in his bed motionless and pretending to be asleep. I knew he couldn't do anything, but I wondered if he felt like I did when it was his turn and I was lying there motionlessly. I was hurt both physically and mentally.

In hindsight, I know I heard my father snoring in the living room. Was he really asleep or was he faking to see if I would forget to show him my clothes? Why not just remind me?

How mean could this man be? I just couldn't understand it. I swear I think he set all of us up on many occasions. I went into the kitchen and set up the ironing board and plugged in the iron. Moving gingerly with every step.

After I had finished ironing my clothes, I gathered myself and went into the living room and showed him my clothes. He was sitting on the couch as if nothing ever happened. As if he didn't just beat the shit out of me.

I wondered if he saw the whelps, bruises and blood on my body and if he did would he show some compassion and try to help me? I am sure he saw it all, but he didn't do anything.

He just said, "Ok now go back to bed." I slowly turned around walked down the hallway to my bedroom.

When I went into the bedroom I turned the light on and Gerald rolled over, looked at me with tears in his eyes and rolled back over. I hung my clothes in the closet and turned off the lights and carefully got in the bed. I felt the pain all the way down to my bones. It was excruciating. It was even hurting with every breath that I took.

As I lay there attempting to sleep, my skin was still burning and I was not able to put the cover on top of me because of the discomfort it caused to my wounds. All kinds of thoughts went through my head. I remember asking myself, "Why was this happening to me?" I don't know which hurt more, my emotions or my body.

My desire to be like my father began to fade with each beating. It not only tore away at my flesh but at my soul.

Like most nights after a beating, I cried myself to sleep that night. I was hurt in ways I couldn't explain. Of course, I would go on to make the same mistakes from time to time unintentionally. As a kid you don't always follow the rules perfectly, not out of defiance but because you're learning about life.

There was no such thing as honest mistakes when it came to my father. No learning curves.

My father's rules were not in place just for me but for my siblings as well. To him, we all had to be punished severely. On a night when my father wasn't abusing me it would be one of my sibling's turn.

There was never a night in that house that my siblings, my mother or I wasn't getting beat by him. Even if it wasn't my turn I still felt their pain, emotionally and mentally.

MAN DOWN

The only time I remember not being beaten for an extended period of time was when my father injured his leg. I found out about the details of my father's injury when I overheard him telling someone that was visiting him at the house. One night my father was entertaining a few guests. After his guests left my father fell asleep on the couch in a drunken stupor. It was about midnight and everyone else in the house was asleep.

My father woke up suddenly because he felt the urge to vomit. He jumped up to run to the bathroom and misjudged the location of the glass table in front of the couch and smashed his leg right into the corner of it.

My mother took my father to the doctor the next morning and the doctor confirmed my father's leg was fractured. The doctor gave my father crutches and pain pills and told him to stay off his leg for a few weeks. Although he was confined to the couch, all of my father's rules still applied. The only change that I noticed was that no one got a whipping for the whole time he was on crutches.

He still argued, fussed and yelled out his orders, but he was in no position to beat anyone. I think my father's injury was God's doing because we definitely got a much-needed break from my father's beatings. My father acted as if he was helpless so we had to wait on him hand and foot. You would think someone that was in need would treat us a little better, but he didn't.

My father constantly ordered us around and demanded things like food, magazines or for someone to turn the channel. I think he did more yelling during his injury than he did when he wasn't injured. The verbal abuse was greater than before.

There was another good thing that came out of his injury. I wasn't scared while I lay in bed at night. I didn't have to worry about hearing the sound of his house shoes slipping and sliding or his belt jingling. The time my father was injured was the best times I have ever had sleeping. He eventually healed after a month and was back to his normal self. I do understand that all good things must come to an end, but this ended too soon.

ANGER MANAGEMENT

I began loving school for reasons other than learning. It became my getaway, my hideout and my comfort place. I was shy and I didn't have any social skills but when reading none of that matters. At school, I would read as many books as the teacher would allow. I considered myself a good student and that was evident by my good grades. As for making friends, if someone reached out to me I would happily accept his or her friendship. Now to initiate any communication or friendship with someone else was not something I could do. I was so used to being alone.

Most of my problems stemmed from home but eventually they started to carry over to the school. I didn't understand why other kids would tick me off so easily. It really didn't take much at all. I was always wound up and ready to pounce on any one.

I was angry all the time. I had no idea that the anger I carried was towards my father. My temper had gotten short and shorter and I began getting into fights at school. To be honest I thought I was a scary kid but I just didn't care anymore.

I didn't realize I had so much rage built up inside of me until it began to show. We had a bully at school and his name was William and nobody liked him. William would fight almost every day and if he weren't fighting it was because the kids were doing what he demanded of them.

One day William picked the wrong day to mess with me. It was recess and I was playing on the Monkey Bars along with the rest of the kids. I stopped playing to watch William pick on this kid. This kid was much smaller than William and very frail. He was crying and it was an image I had seen too many times in my own house.

William looked at me and asked what I was looking at? I was in no mood to deal with his bullying especially when I had a bully at home four times the size of him that bullied me 24/7. If I could take my father's beatings then what kind of beatings could a kid my size give me? So I responded right back to William, "I'm looking at you!" I think he was a little surprised to hear someone stand up to him. In fact, it seemed as if the whole schoolyard was surprised.

William came over to where I was standing with his fists clenched. It didn't faze me one bit as I had a mean look on my face as well. We were standing face to face and the other kids were crowding around us. Before we could do anything, the ground monitor stepped in and told us to break it up. That would be the start of many of my battles with William. He and I would fight many times after school and during school with me losing every single time.

To most I may have lost, but I considered myself a winner. One reason was that William no longer picked on anyone else in the school. He was quite too busy pounding on me.

The other reason is that little did he or anyone know, our fights allowed me to let out a little aggression. So in all, I actually felt I won every single time. Although it was William that I was physically fighting, mentally it was my dad.

I actually liked William, he was a lot like me. He was an angry and confused kid. I wondered if he too had a father like mine? It was too bad we couldn't be friends and talk about it. Over time, I managed to get William's respect and the respect of all my other schoolmates. I may have lost every fight, but William knew that with me, he was getting just that, a fight.

ON THE ROCKS

I had finally graduated from Mark Twain Elementary School in September of 1976. I was 12 years old. The following summer was going to be extremely long, as it meant no school. There was nothing in the way that would interfere with the duties that my father planned for Gerald and I.

The fence was already done, the entire pavement was laid and everything looked great. Yet my father was far from done. My father bought a white birdbath that was three feet high and it was shaped like an open flower. He placed it in the center of the lawn. It was nice and no one else in the neighborhood had one. He made sure we kept fresh water in the birdbath at all times. We also had a flowerbed right by the front door, but we didn't have any flowers planted there.

He bought tons of white crystal rocks and brown beauty barks and put them in the flowerbed.

Beauty barks were basically small chips of wood. This had to have been the neatest flowerbed I have ever seen. My father made us clean it out once a month.

When it was time to clean the flowerbed, it was more like a punishment. One Saturday he had all of us cleaning out the flowerbed. It was not just the boys this time but the girls as well. First we had to remove all the rocks and beauty barks from the flowerbed.

After removing the rocks and beauty barks, we had to pull up every weed we saw in the dirt and then level the dirt. Once we pulled out all the weeds and leveled the dirt, we then had to carefully place the beauty barks back onto the dirt.

They were carefully placed on the dirt because we had to spread them out evenly and not on top of each other. Once the beauty barks were in place, it was time to lay the rocks down.

We had to dip each rock into a bucket of soapy water that we prepared, clean them and then dry them off one by one. We then had to gently place them back into the dirt. If we had gotten any of the rocks dirty he would make us take them back out the dirt, dip them in water again, dry them off and place them back into the dirt.

I couldn't tell you exactly how many white rocks there were, but my guess would have been over a thousand rocks.

My back was killing me for being bent over for hours with no break in-between. Not only was this task grueling but it also was humiliating to all of us.

I speak on behalf of all my siblings when I say it was pure hell. Our friends were slowly walking past our house, some laughing and some in disbelief that my father had us doing such a menial chore.

I wish I could have crawled under one of those rocks. In a way, I was happy that school was out for the summer because had school been in I would have been a joke for the day.

There were many days I knew I would never forget as long as I lived and this was one of them.

SPLIT PERSONALITY

My father's taste was exquisite in every aspect of the word. It didn't matter what it was but if it had something to do with him it had to be lavish.

I couldn't believe he was driving an old classic station wagon as long as he has. It was light green and had wood grain panels on the sides and a glass roof at the top.

At the time, it was our everyday vehicle that he and my mom shared. I guess the station wagon eventually cramped his style because he went out and bought a brand new 1969 Buick Riviera. It was a sweet car.

It was light brown with tan leather interior and stock alloy rims. He wouldn't allow my mother to drive it or any of us to ride in it. We were limited to the station wagon, which was the vehicle my mother drove to run errands for her and my father.

My father always dressed up and went out while my mother stayed home with us. I had no problem with that as long as he was gone I was happy.

My mother didn't seem to have an issue with it either but even if she did I don't think she would voice it to him in fear of backlash. We seemed to have so much fun when my father wasn't there. My mom wouldn't let us get too far out of line because she knew my father would get her and us.

My mom was scared of my father. She would smile a lot when he wasn't there but when he was around she wouldn't smile at all. She also stayed out of his way. I'm certain she didn't like the way he treated her children, but at the same time she definitely feared for her own safety.

She was a good wife and always a good mother to all of her children. Regardless of how good my mother was to my father he constantly yelled and fussed at my mother and treated her with very little respect.

There were times I witnessed him getting mad at my mom and chasing her around the house. She would run all through the house to keep him from hitting her. Eventually, he would catch her and hit her not caring that her kids were watching.

I've witnessed times when he would verbally degrade her by yelling really loud, telling her she was stupid, dumb and ignorant. My mom would just take it and cry.

During an argument if she tried to explain her side of the story my father would consider that back talking, which instantly ticked him off and he would hit her causing bruises.

This was something I witnessed way too often and one of the saddest things I saw.

The times that I witnessed my father physically abusing my mother I could see the embarrassment in my mother's eyes. She had to have been a strong woman to endure such humiliation and physical abuse, but I'm sure my mother's spirit was broken a long time ago.

There were many questions I've always wanted to ask my mom. I wanted to ask her, "why does he hit you, why does he beat us and why don't you stop him from hurting us?"

I think my siblings and I chose not to ask my mother such questions because she had already endured so much abuse from my father so we kept quiet. My father was clever in how he dealt with people outside of the house. To them, he was charismatic, charming, entertaining and fun to be around.

That was the man I wanted to be like, not the man that his wife and children knew. It seemed as if everyone else liked him. Either that or they were too afraid to confront him on his wrong doings. I am sure many of them knew how he was treating his family.
Unfortunately, no one had the heart or compassion to do anything about it. My father had dinner parties and invited family and friends over to join him. Whenever he did he would tell Gerald and I to clean the yard and have my sisters clean the house while my mother cooked. This was one of the times we didn't mind working.

We knew that when he had company he would not pay any attention to us.

Whenever he entertained guests, we were able to go outside and play with the children that came over with them. This was one of the times we actually felt normal. My siblings and I were happy. We didn't know when we would have another moment like this and at that time we didn't care.

Whenever guests came over to the house, he became a man unknown to us. He was totally in disguise.

I was always the observant and curious type. I went inside the house to get some water and as I was walking past everyone I got a glance of a man my father would morph into. He would turn into the father I never had.

He was the center of attention and everyone was laughing at his jokes. He looked very happy. I thought this would be a great time to see if my father would be nice to me. I wanted my father to show he cared about me and that he loved me, even if he was pretending in front of everyone.

I made sure to walk slowly while I was looking at him. I even had a smile on my face. I was hoping he would call me in front of all of his guests and ask me to do something for him but in a nice way. My father noticed me all right. He stopped smiling long enough to shush me right out the house. He couldn't even muster up something nice to say to me even if it wasn't real.

He didn't care that he was in front of all these people and in a great mood.

As I was hurrying towards the door, I looked at my mother laughing and smiling with the women. This was different as I rarely saw this beautiful smile on my mother's face.

My father even hugged my mother in front of everyone. I am sure it wasn't real, but it made her happy. Wow, what a picture I thought to myself. My parents were laughing and the kids were outside playing. You know, from the outside looking in you would think we were the happiest family on the block.

As the night grew old and my father's guests went home, we knew the fun was over and everything would go back to normal. There would be no laughing or smiling.

The air would again be filled with fear, my father's shouting voice and our painful cries. Watching each guest leave one by one was hard. After the last guest was gone we had to clean up the mess left behind.

Each of my siblings was assigned kitchen duty a week at a time. So whoever had kitchen duty on days when he had company was in for a long night. Well, it just happened to be my week. It seemed like it took me forever to get the kitchen cleaned. They practically used every dish in the house. I needed some help but unless my father suggested it we had to do it by ourselves. When I was finished, I think it was around eleven o'clock that evening.

Everyone else was asleep including my father. He was in his favorite spot in the living room snoring. I turned off the lights in the kitchen and went to my room. I thought to myself, I had a nice day today and to top it off no beatings.

I lay down and before I closed my eyes, I ran all the chores through my mind making sure I didn't forget anything before I went to sleep. Before I closed my eyes I thought to myself, this was not a bad day at all.

THE PROMISE

It was a Sunday and I heard my family in the kitchen cooking breakfast led by none other than my father. I took the cover off my head and looked to see if it was light outside.

It was light out, but it had to be around six in the morning and as usual my father was fussing and cursing. I turned over and put the cover over my head and tried to drown out the yelling, but that didn't work. A few minutes later my father came to our room and ordered my brother and I to get up and clean the yard. We jumped up and got dressed.

When we walked through the kitchen, I saw my mother and sisters working like slaves. My father was yelling and shouting out orders. As I was headed out the back door, my father stopped me and said, "What did I tell you about not emptying the trash before going to bed?" All I could say was I forgot. He said, "Well I'm not going to forget to whip your ass so know you have that coming". Then he told me to take out the trash. I emptied the trash and began to clean around the yard.

Normally I would be happy when he called us in for breakfast but because the beating was on my mind my appetite was not there.

After working in the yard for about an hour, we were called inside to come eat. When we went inside the house, I washed my hands, went to the table and began eating. The food didn't have a taste to it.

All I tasted was fear. The taste of fear was a taste I was all too familiar with, but I could never explain it. The closer I got to finishing my food, the more afraid I became.

My father was watching T.V. and I thought he was waiting on me to finish. I was pretty sure this was the time I was going to get my beating. As I put my plate away I anticipated that he would call me but he didn't. I walked down the hallway that I nicknamed the hallway of death.

I called it that because of the way my father would slip and slide down the hallway on his way to whip me. The other reason I called it that is because it seems like forever to get out of harms way and safely to my room. I went into my room and just waited.

I picked up a book, sat on my bed and attempted to read it, but I couldn't concentrate.

I put the book down and just sat there on my bed looking at the bare white walls. I thought if I stayed out of his sight I might stay out of his mind. While I sat waiting in my room, every sound I heard startled me.

Whoever walked down the hallway or whenever Gerald would come into the room, my heart would skip a beat.

Other than trying to avoid getting a beating there were a couple of reasons why I preferred to be in my room. One is that watching T.V. with my father was terrible.

Whenever we watched T.V. with my father, we had to watch everything that he wanted to watch. There was nothing he watched that we liked. He was a sport fanatic and I remember watching boxing, football and basketball. We watched sports with him so much that his favorite teams ultimately became my favorite teams. The other reason I didn't like watching T.V. with my father was because I felt if I were nearby it would remind my father that he owed me a whipping.

I was definitely not interested in reminding him that he owes me a beating so staying in my room staring at the walls was just fine for me. I stayed in my room from 12:30 p.m. until 5:00 p.m.

I couldn't hide any longer because my mother called me so that I could eat dinner. My father didn't eat with us, he ate in the living room.

It was quiet at the table and everyone knew I was going to get a beating. It was like the quiet before the storm. No one appeared to be in a good mood. After dinner, it was time for me to clean up the kitchen. The time was getting closer for me to face my father. This time I remembered to take out the trash.

When I came back inside from taking out the trash, I noticed he was not on the couch anymore. So my first thought was that he went to go get an extension cord. My heart began pounding.

I put the trashcan down and walked to my room to get some clothes so I could hurry and take a bath. I went back to the bathroom and ran my bath water. There were times I hated taking baths, mostly because after my beatings the water would make my wounds burn.

So sometimes I would pretend to take baths. This time I wanted to take a bath for as long as I could. While I was taking a bath, I heard my father come inside the house. He must have been in the garage this whole time or gone somewhere.

I was a nervous wreck. I knew I couldn't stay in the bathroom forever so I let the water out of the bathtub and got dressed and went into my room. After entering my room, my father yelled out my name.

My heart started beating so fast that I thought it was going to explode. The fear I had tasted all day had gotten stronger.

I made my way down the hallway of death and I went in the living room to get my beating. He said, "I want you to know I didn't forget to beat your ass for not taking out the trash, but I'm not going to whip you this time, but next time I am." I couldn't believe what I was hearing. I am sure I had this dumbfounded look on my face.

Deep inside I was doing a happy dance and it took everything for me not to smile.

To my knowledge my father has never let us slide with anything. I began to tear up and I don't know why. A second ago I was happy. Now I'm tearing up. I don't know if the tears were tears of gratitude, or if it was that since noon that day I had been beat mentally and was glad it was finally over.

My father asked me a question that caught me off guard. He said, "Do you think I should have whipped you?" The craziest, most asinine thing came out of my mouth. I answered, "Yes". I mean who asks a kid that in the first place? I figured my father's question was a test or trick so I wanted him to know I felt whipped already.

If I had answered no would I have failed the test? My father laughed and told me to go to bed. Without hesitation, I briskly walked away.

As I made my way down the hall of death, I was trying to make sense of what just happened. I am not sure, but I think he actually showed some care.

I don't know, but it was the closest thing to care I have felt from him. I was confused. My father had never hugged me, never patted me on the back and never told me that he loved me. When he didn't whip me I guess I took that as some type of affection.

Whatever it was I'd take it. I went to sleep that night wondering if I was being setup. My father just doesn't do nice things for his kids. It's unfortunate that his kids couldn't differentiate his good actions from his bad actions.

FLASHLIGHT

Weekdays were like weekends for us during the summer. I say that because on weekends we had to get up, get dressed and clean the yard. Now that it was summer we were doing this every single day. My father's work hours changed because he started working for a new trucking company. His new shift started at 6:00 p.m. That meant he was home during the day. He made us work with him as he conquered many different projects.

I remember Gerald and I was helping my father put up a cabinet in the kitchen. It was a project I wouldn't forget. My father had just put the finishing touches on a cabinet he built to hang from the ceiling. It was on the floor and he needed someone to hold the flashlight for him so he could see inside of the cabinet while he hammered. He called out for one of us to get a flashlight and shine it so he could see.

Gerald and I hesitated a little because we knew that holding a flashlight for my father was not a simple task. My father would have you holding the flashlight in one spot forever and the flashlight better not move.

So I waited for Gerald to move and Gerald waited for me. My father yelled, "Hurry up got dam it!!" Unfortunately for Gerald he was closer to the hammer than I was. So Gerald nervously picked up the flashlight and looked back at me in anger and fear. I smiled, but I didn't smile long because I didn't want my father to catch me.

Gerald was holding the flashlight for about 10 minutes. My father was taking a long time and he appeared to be having some issues. I could see Gerald was getting tired of holding the flashlight because his arm was trembling. I thought to myself oh -oh, this is not going to be good.

Gerald thought quickly and switched hands without moving the flashlight and a sigh of relief went over me. I don't know what problem my father was having, but he didn't seem to be in a rush. Gerald's other arm began tiring so again he switched back to his right hand. Only this time while switching hands, Gerald took the flashlight off the target and my father yelled, "Keep the fucking light still!!" I could tell my father was getting angry because he was already irritated by the problems he was having with the cabinet. At this point, Gerald was not only tired but also scared and that made him tremble more.

This is exactly why I didn't want to hold the flashlight for my father. My father directed Gerald to hold the flashlight at a certain angle, periodically changing from angle to angle. This one time Gerald held it at the wrong angle and my father got pissed.

My father was accustomed to swinging when he was angry and that is exactly what he did. The problem with that was, he was holding a hammer in his hand while he was swinging.

Without looking, my father cursed and quickly swung the hammer behind him and almost took Gerald's head off. It was a good thing Gerald was able to move just enough because my father missed Gerald's head by inches.

My father must have realized he acted without thinking because he immediately dropped the hammer before he swung again. He connected with the side of Gerald's head with his fist this time and said, "Now dam it hold the fucking light like I told you to". Gerald held the flashlight as steady as he could while tearing up. I was pissed.

I couldn't believe how close he came to hitting my brother in the head with that hammer. This was the first time I actually wanted to harm my father. I wanted to pick up the same hammer and bash my father over the head with it. However, the thought went away as quickly as it came because I knew my father would kill me.

Finally, my father figured out the issue he was having with the cabinet and we were done. Still teary-eyed Gerald put down the flashlight.

When it was time to attach the cabinet to the ceiling, my father gave Gerald some anchors to take into the crawl space above. He directed Gerald to drop the screws through the holes that were pre-drilled.

I have looked in the attic before and all I saw was insulation, spider webs and Lord knows what else.

I assumed my father chose Gerald to go because I was a lot bigger than Gerald and he would be able to maneuver better in tight spaces. Without hesitation, Gerald went into the crawl space. I actually wanted to go in the crawl space myself after witnessing the hammer incident.

I think Gerald was glad to go up there too and I don't think even spiders could have deterred him from going.

Gerald climbed into the attic and followed my father's instructions of where to drop the bolts down. Meanwhile, my father was showing me how to grab one end of the cabinet and walk up the ladder at the same time.

The cabinet was almost the same size as I was so it took a lot of work getting it up to the ceiling. It was a good thing it was pretty light.

There was no way my father was going to go for me not being able to lift it. To my surprise I did it. Once we got it to the ceiling, my father yelled for Gerald to drop the bolts down. I guess Gerald was having a hard time dropping the bolts down initially and my father began yelling and screaming.

I was getting tired and hoping Gerald would drop the bolts down in the right place because if he didn't I would be in trouble next.

Every part of my body was in pure agony as I tried to hold the cabinet in place.

I began to tremble and I was ready to be my father's next victim. My body felt on the verge of giving up. I couldn't hold it any longer. This was too much for a kid.

Gerald finally was able to get all the bolts in and my father told him to hold them while he tightened them. Gerald had been in the attic for a while now and let me remind you that this was during the summer time.

It was 88 degrees outside and even hotter in the crawl space with very little ventilation. My father eventually tightened all the bolts and Gerald was allowed to come back down. I was relieved and very sore.

When Gerald came down from the crawl space, he was covered in spider webs from head to toe and drenched in sweat. What was crazy to me is that Gerald had a smile on his face.

I guess it was his way of teasing me because I was stuck down here with my father. To him he was safely in the attic. He immediately went to get some water, and then to the bathroom to clean up. As bad as he looked I would have traded positions with him at any time, just as long as I wasn't too close to my dad.

Working with my father was very unpredictable.

I understand learning early but with my father it was hard to learn because there were no learning curves. So being within arms length of him is never a good thing.

THE GOOD SEED

The summer of 1975 couldn't end fast enough for me. Most kids look forward to the summer because there's no school, lots of swimming and they were able to sleep in. We didn't get to do any of that. Summers with my father were more for him than us. I missed my friends from school and at this point I even missed fighting William.

All the kids around us were playing and enjoying their time off from school and we were working harder than ever. There was no explanation for why we had to work so hard at home. We cleaned the house and yard every single day. When we weren't doing house chores we stayed in our rooms.

I couldn't understand how the yard needed to be cleaned up every day. Grass or weeds didn't grow back that fast. To be honest, there was no work to be done. It was as if he hated to see us not doing anything. He literally made up things for us to do daily. Normally spring-cleaning was once a month if that. Now that it is summer, it seems as though it was every weekend.

He had us cleaning the walls, ceiling, pulling out all the dishes in the kitchen and wiping down the inside and outside of the cabinets.

We cleaned the baseboards and corners of the floors and the garbage cans in the yard. It was rare that we had a chance to play during the summer. That would depend on if my father were home or not. If he weren't home my mother would allow us to relax. We couldn't go out the yard because she didn't know exactly when my father would turn the corner.

Sometimes my father came home for lunch in his big rig. Whenever he came home for lunch, we had to pretend we were working. It was a good thing he was in his truck because we heard him coming from far away.

I remember counting the seconds when it was time for him to go back to work. It seems like the only reason he came home was to use the restroom. He would come home and go straight to the restroom and stay in there for 45 minutes to an hour.

That was nearly all of his lunchtime. During that time, we worked doing things my mother told us to do. As soon as my father left we all went back to playing. I usually played with Gerald but sometimes Sharon, Gerald and I would play together.

We would just laugh and make up silly games. I remember one time Gerald, Sharon and I were outside in the back yard. There was a tree near the boy's room. The tree had dropped dry, crusty leaves on the ground.

We decided we were going to make a cigarette and smoke it like my parents do. So we put some leaves inside this piece of paper that we'd found on the ground and we rolled the paper into a cigarette. Gerald had some matches that he snuck out of the house and we lit it. We took turns pretending to smoke the cigarette but didn't know how to inhale.

We sucked on the rolled up paper and leaves and pretended we were blowing out the smoke. That was the only time we did anything like that. It kind of felt good to involve Sharon in our little mischief because she was the golden child in the family. I wanted Sharon to do other bad things with me and get caught. I was always jealous of the relationship she had with my father. After some thought, I realized it wouldn't be a good idea.

My father would probably think I put her up to it and that his precious daughter had fallen from grace because of me. It seemed like she could do no wrong in my father's eyes. She never got in trouble, whipped, or even yelled at. All I remember is my father babying her and laughing with her. This infuriated me because I felt I didn't do anything wrong either. All I wanted was to be loved and treated as if he liked me. One day my father had this nice stereo cabinet in the living room. It was big, brown and lacquered with a wet bar on one side and a stereo and record player on the other.

Directly below the stereo and record player was an electrically simulated fireplace. My father played music a lot.

He sang and danced by himself often. He looked so funny to me. He would stick his tongue out and put it to the side of his mouth. Then he would snap his fingers loudly and did a whole lot of stepping. My father was as stiff as a board and never used his hips. One of his favorite songs was "My Cherie Amour" by Stevie Wonder. He would grab my sister Sharon and dance with her while serenading her as she smiled.

This always had me steaming mad at Sharon. Another song my father loved was "Daddy's Home" by the Delfonics. My father made all of us get together and sing to him. He sang the verses and we sang the chorus. It was not something we wanted to do. Well, no one but Sharon but regardless we had no choice. We pretended to like it and did what he said, but that song was definitely not our song.

My father seemed to be in a good mood when he was drinking. He wasn't really the type of man who got angry or any meaner than he already was just because he was drinking. It was rare to see him in a light mood when he was amongst just us. Some would probably think his drinking is what caused him to be as mean as he was but actually it made him nicer.

MY SAVIOR

Out of all my uncles and aunts, my favorite aunt was my father's sister Edna. I remember a showdown she had with my father one day.

On this particular day, my siblings and I were all in the living room sitting on the floor watching TV. There were times when we preferred to be in our room, but my father would make us watch T.V. with him.

The floor in the living room was very uncomfortable. It was floor tile on the floor and underneath the tile was concrete.

My father didn't allow us to use blankets or pillows. He also didn't allow any of us to lie down when we were watching T.V. We had to sit Indian style for hours. There were times when I'd fall asleep sitting and when he noticed it he would yell from the couch and say, "Michael, wake your ass up". My back used to kill me from sitting on the hard, cold, tile in the same position for hours at a time.

I would rather sit and watch the walls in my bedroom than to be in the living room with my father.

On this Saturday afternoon when we were watching T.V., my auntie knocked on the door and she and Uncle Lee walked right into the house before anyone could say come in.

This was how my aunt Edna made her entrance. She never waited for anyone to say come in. As soon as she came through the door she said, "Jack let these damn kids go outside. It's nice outside and you got them sitting up here watching T.V." My father said, "Shut the hell up you're not raising my kids I am".

They went back and forth for a while with my aunt not backing down a bit. My aunt told my father, "You can't kick my ass muthafucka. I am not one of your got damn kids". My Aunt Edna then turned to my mother and said with a laugh, "Marla why aren't these kids outside playing like regular kids, are they on a punishment again. I have never seen kids be on punishment so damn much".

My mother looked at my aunt and smiled and said, "You know how Jack is". My father got agitated and said to my aunt, "Your kids are in Carson if you want to go raise some kids you have eight of your own". My father and aunt went back and forth for a few minutes. We knew not to look back at either one of them and to pretend we weren't hearing anything.

My father said, "Don't be talking this shit in front of my kids like that Edna".

He then told us to go outside until he called us back inside the house. I was surprised he let us go outside.

I thought if anything, he would make us go to our rooms, but I think he knew my aunt would stay on him about keeping us cooped up in the house.

My siblings and I went outside quickly and did not look back. As I was leaving the house I heard my father and aunt arguing and I knew that was my aunt's way of temporarily releasing us. My mother and Uncle would just sit back and laugh. Uncle Lee had a passive aggressive personality. He was laid back, col and always use to crack jokes.

He was 5'11, had a dark brown complexion and thick black hair. He always wore dark rimmed eyeglasses and jeans with a plaid shirt. Uncle lee always made me laugh because after telling a joke he would laugh harder than anyone else. I would say he and Aunt Edna was a real live odd couple. She found herself a great man in Uncle Lee. None of her eight children were his, but he married her and treated each one as if they were.

ALL SCREWED UP

My father came up with the idea of building a shed in the backyard to store his tools and miscellaneous items. My father made us help him build a wooden 8x8 shed that was elevated from the ground to keep it from flooding when it rained. There was nothing special about the shed just four walls, flat ceiling and a floor. There were no windows.

Building the shed was actually easy. Gerald and I were in charge of sawing the lumber after my father measured and marked it. We had to drill screws where he told us to drill them. The thing Gerald and I learned at such young ages!

It took us close to a week to build the shed. When we finished building the shed my father immediately told us to store all sorts of items into the shed. We loaded the shed to seventy five percent of its capacity with items that had been stored in the garage.

The shed became another source for my father to send us to when he needed us to look for something or put something away. My father was extremely anal when it came to finding things.

When he sent us to find something, it didn't matter how long it took. We were not allowed to stop looking for anything until it was found. In his mind, he knew for a fact that the item was there but that we didn't look good enough. I will never forget one particular Friday afternoon around 3:00 p.m. My father went into the shed to look for a screw and he couldn't find it. He called for Gerald and I and instructed us to look for it.

He gave us an identical screw and told us to go inside the shed and find the screw that looked like the one he gave us. He told us he was sure it was inside the shed. So with the screw in my hand Gerald and I went inside the shed to look for the screw.

We didn't think much about the request because it was a typical type of request given by my father on any given day. If my father wasn't asking us to get something out of the shed, then he was asking us to get something out of the garage or house.

Gerald and I went inside the shed and looked inside most of the boxes, cans and toolboxes. We searched for the screw for about thirty minutes and couldn't find it. We went back to my father and told him we couldn't find it. My father was livid. He yelled at us and said, "You didn't look long enough get back out there and don't come back in this house till you find it". Gerald and I hurried out of the house and back to the shed to look for the screw. This time we took every box we could lift out of the shed and systematically looked through them.

Again we found nothing. There were other boxes that were too heavy for us to lift so we had to practically take everything out of those boxes to make sure the screw wasn't in them.

The screw appeared to be a standardly sized screw, but we couldn't find it. We came across plenty of screws that may have worked, but we knew my father wanted this particular screw. We had been in the shed for two hours now and we were getting upset because we couldn't find anything.

Suddenly I heard a voice that was music to my ears. It was my mother calling for Gerald and I to come eat dinner. It must have been around 5:00 p.m. because that was our usual dinnertime. I was relieved because I was not only hungry but also tired. When we went inside the house, we didn't see my father.

I assumed he was either in the room or the garage. Just when we were about to sit down for dinner my father came into the house. He asked us if we had found the screw that he told us to look for. In harmony, Gerald and I said, "No".

My father said, "Well why in the hell are y'all in this fucking house?" Obviously he didn't know my mother had called us in to eat dinner. My mother chimed in and said, "I called them in to eat dinner". My father interrupted my mother and said, "I don't give a fuck". He turned and looked at us and said, "Get the fuck out of this house and I don't care what anybody says, you do not come in here again until you find that fucking screw".

We rushed out the house as if we were being chased. He could have been chasing us, but neither one us would have ever known because we never looked back. I could hear my father say to my mother "Don't you ever call them in here for shit else".

My mother said, "But they haven't eaten at least let them eat first". My father said, "I don't give a fuck if they never eat".

He stuck his head out the door and yelled at us again and said, "Do not come in this fucking house unless you have that screw and I don't care if its tomorrow".

I don't know about Gerald, but I was steaming mad. I was running and stomping hard. I remember thinking to myself this man is crazy and I hated him for how he was treating us. I appreciated my mother for trying to get us inside the house to eat dinner, but I am glad she didn't get in trouble herself.

Gerald and I began searching the same boxes that we had searched many times before. It was like looking for a needle in a haystack. A couple of hours had passed and we were still looking through boxes in the shed. The sun was starting to go down and soon it was going to be even harder to find that screw. I definitely didn't want to be out here while it was dark and cold.

So I sped up my search and looked under anything I could in hopes to find it. Gerald and I had not eaten since earlier this morning and I am sure he was starving because I certainly was. Several hours had passed and now it was dark outside.

We really couldn't find the screw although we looked in each container and box, over and over.

I looked at Gerald and saw how worn down he was and shaking from the cold temperature. We didn't have jackets on because we were rushed out of the house when the weather was still warm. I was cold and doing a little shaking myself. I probably would have been even colder if I weren't steaming mad.

I had thoughts of running away, but I knew Gerald wouldn't go with me and I didn't want to leave him alone. I had so many thoughts going through my head and most of them didn't even make any sense but I didn't care.

One thought I had in mind was going to my father and telling him to beat my ass and get it over with. Up until now, none of my father's beatings seemed worse than what Gerald and I were going through in that shed. Going back into the house and facing my father would not only put me at risk of my father's abuse but my brother as well.

I didn't like that Gerald was involved because of his subdued and timid personality. I always felt like I was Gerald's older brother opposed to it being the other way around.

I could take all that my father had to dish out, but I knew Gerald couldn't. The smart person inside of me knew better than to confront my father, but the bad person in me was gaining momentum.

On that night, in the shed I really started to notice my two personalities.

One personality was calm, intelligent, creative and respectful. The other personality was the one that my father created, which was mean, selfish, thoughtless and heartless.

As a young child, I knew I had some edginess to me but I didn't consider myself a mean person. I know 12 years old isn't old but I could see more and more of my father's mean spirit.

Maybe I was more like my father than I had realized. Maybe he saw himself in me and that is what he didn't like. Maybe, for that reason I became the source of his rage.

Many hours had passed and my father never came outside to ask us if we had found the screw or suggest that we look again tomorrow. I'm sure it was past our bedtime. Our energy was drained as well as our spirits. We actually stopped looking for the screw. We had looked in every square inch of that shed and in every box, crate and bucket.

I think it was about 10:30 p.m. or later and our bedtime was 9:00 p.m. I knew my mother was worried sick about us. She knew we didn't have jackets and that her babies had not eaten since this morning. It's crazy because I was the one that was outside freezing, tired and hungry yet there I was worried about my mother. Again the thought crossed my mind as to why my mother didn't stop this abuse by my father.

I never blamed my mother, but I always wondered what was going on in her head at the time.

Quickly I would remind myself that she too was being mistreated by my father and was scared of him.

Gerald and I didn't say much to each other while we were going through this ordeal. There was nothing to be said. It was like we both were in deep thought.

So many emotions were coming and going. Over time, I had gone from tired to sleepy.

We walked around as if we were zombies. Occasionally we would look for the screw whenever we heard a sound and thought our father was coming. I think that was the first time I wished he would come and do whatever he had to do and get it over with. My clothes began to dampen from the dew that normally sets in at night.

Mentally I had already given up. I was broken and I didn't care too much. I was sleepy, cold and hungry. I told Gerald I was going inside our room through the bedroom window to get some sleep. I told him I could barely keep my eyes open.

I asked if he would look out for me and wake me if he heard something and that I would do the same for him when it was his turn. Gerald was having no part of it.

Like I said, he was very timid and the scary type. I, on the other hand, took more chances. Gerald told me that he would not look out for me and told me not to climb into the window.

He said, "If daddy sees you he is going to beat you." I told him that I didn't care and that it was a chance I'd have to take.

So against my brother's warnings, I climbed into the window and onto my bed. I knew I had to be very quiet. My father mostly slept in the living room so I didn't think he would hear me.

I had no fear, no care and no feelings. I was emotionally drained. Gerald was probably afraid of him, but I sure wasn't. I couldn't have been sleep for more than five minutes when Gerald came to the window and whispered, "Michael, Michael come on I hear something". I immediately jumped up and practically dove out of the window headfirst. My heart was beating extremely fast. I ran to the shed and we pretended to look for the screw. Just a few minutes ago I was fearless and ready to take the beast head on. I guess that was delirium because I was terrified.

After a few minutes, I realized it was a false alarm. I really don't think Gerald heard anything at all.

I think he was just scared for my life and his. He knew that if my father caught me in that room and Gerald hadn't told him, he would have beaten the living daylights out of both of us. For the rest of the night and into the morning, our routine was to pretend we were looking for the screw whenever we thought we heard something.

I'm guessing it was 4:00 a.m. when I began to hear the birds chirping. Dew had set in on just about everything that didn't move and it was freezing cold.

We had been deprived of food for so long that hunger was no longer our issue.

We were leaning on boxes, crates, boards or against walls trying to prop ourselves up while we dozed from time to time. Again, at this point I didn't care if we got caught or not. Over and over I thought how could he do this to us? Gerald and I were only twelve and thirteen years old. How was he able to sleep leaving his two young sons out in the cold with no water, food, proper clothing or sleep?

My views of my father had changed dramatically as a result of the treatment we had gotten today. My father was no longer the man I thought I wanted to be like.

Going through this horrible ordeal in the shed convinced me that my father didn't like me. To think at one time I actually wanted him to like me. I often wondered if I had done something to make him feel this way towards me. What could I do to be the son he wanted me to be? All my siblings knew I was the one that he seemed to target the most. There wasn't any way I could have been a bad child because if I had gotten out of line my father would abruptly put me back in my place. I felt my father was intentionally destroying my self-esteem. I was beginning to dislike my life or myself and I began to rethink running away.

As I sat on a box nodding off and on for what seemed like an hour, I noticed that the sun was coming up. I figured it must have been 5:30 a.m. or 6:00 a.m.

It was good to see the sunlight because we needed to thaw out and look for the screw once again. Maybe, just maybe, we could find that screw. It was obvious my father had no intention of calling off the search and I don't think I could make it through another day.

Although it was now morning, there was still no sign of my father. We'd been out here for over thirteen hours and he had not checked on us in any way. We could have been killed back here or kidnapped for all he knew, but he didn't care one bit.

As the sun rose, Gerald and I started looking for the screw. We intended to really find it this time. We tried to have a little pep in our step, but our aching bodies slowed our movements. We spent another couple of hours looking for the screw. At this point, I expected one of two things to happen.

Either my father would find out we didn't find the screw and would tell us to go in the house, or he would find out we didn't find the screw and start beating us.

I was prepared for either scenario. I figured what could be worse? We had an older neighbor named Pete, which worked on cars in his backyard. Pete was the neighborhood mechanic. Pete was chubby, dark skinned and wore overalls twenty-four seven. He pretty much looked like a typical mechanic.

That morning, Pete was getting ready to work on some cars in his yard and he heard Gerald and I rummaging through the boxes in the shed.

He peeked through the gate and said, "Hey what are y'all doing up so early, what are y'all looking for?"

We told him we were looking for a screw that our father wanted us to find. He asked us how long we had been looking for it.

We told him that we'd been looking since last night. Pete said, "So you mean to tell me that y'all been looking for this screw since yesterday evening and he had y'all get up early in the morning and look again?"

We told him that we had been out here looking every since yesterday evening and had not yet been in the house. I could tell my neighbor was both disturbed and a little confused. He said, "Wait a minute, you mean to tell me y'all been out here since yesterday evening looking for a dam screw? Are you fucking kidding me?" Pete looked upset and disgusted. We confirmed that what we had told him was the truth. He said, "So you guys have not been to sleep and have not eaten since yesterday evening?" We said, "Nope".

A look of disbelief came over his face. In an angry tone Pete said, "What do the screw look like?" We gave him the screw and he told us he would be right back.

He got into his car and drove down the alley behind our house. He came back about thirty minutes later, got out of his car and came to the fence and said, "Here, now take it to him…don't worry I scratched the screw up a bit and rolled it in some dirt so he'll never know the difference".

He also had given us each a small hamburger and told us to hurry up and eat them.

We ate the burgers as if we hadn't eaten in weeks. We were happy for what Pete did for us and knew our search was over. After eating, we put away all the boxes that we had taken out of the shed and took the screw to my father. My father was lying on the couch watching T.V. and drinking some coffee. I told my father that we found the screw and I held my hand out to show him.

He asked us where did we find the screw? We told him that it was at the bottom of a huge box with a lot of other loose stuff. It was hard to see because it had gotten dark. My father responded that he knew the screw was in the shed and that is why he wasn't going to let us tell him that it wasn't.

He also said, "You have to look for it, it's not going to jump in your face. So from now on, don't tell me you can't find something without looking".

Gerald and I just said, "okay". My father told us to get cleaned up and to get ready for breakfast. I was so elated.

I couldn't believe the trick worked. I was so exhausted that food was not what I needed. I needed to sleep.

This was one time I wish he sent me to my room for a week. Instead, we had to go get cleaned up and get ready for breakfast.

The one thing that stayed with me throughout this whole ordeal was that my father never checked on us.

I couldn't believe he was that cruel to leave us outside all night. That was a dark day that I could never shine any light on. My thoughts and feelings towards my father would be forever changed. That night in the shed made me stronger, but I didn't know if that would be for better or for worse.

SOUL PAIN LINE

I realized my father was a very stubborn and selfish man. At times, I thought I would get a chance to see a glimpse of my father's caring side but that was only wishful thinking. I thought the house, cars and other nice things that my father bought were because he wanted his family to live comfortably, but I slowly realized it wasn't for us at all. It was all just a show for him and those he wanted to impress.

My father would buy and do things for himself first and it would be the best of the best. He was very concerned about having a youthful appearance. Whatever my father didn't spend on himself was the only time he gave to his family.

It wasn't as if we weren't worthy of the same things he bought for himself, but that's how he treated us. For instance, my father ate things that we were not allowed to eat.

I remember his favorite cookies were Lorna Doones shortbread cookies. He use to send us to the store to get those cookies all the time and all we could do was look at them not eat them.

My father had a lot of favorites such as steaks, ice cream, fruit cocktails and peaches. You name it, he ate it and we couldn't. One day my father sent Gerald and I to get him a double scoop of coconut pineapple ice cream. We got it from the local drug store called Clark Drugs that was just down the street.

My father gave us thirty cents to get a double scoop of ice cream. Gerald and I went to the store, bought an ice cream and hurried home to give it to my father. It took us about twenty minutes. Right before we got to the house we noticed the ice cream was melting.

We didn't think anything of it other than to hurry and get it in the house before it melted all the way. When we gave the ice cream to my father, he was very upset because the ice cream had melted onto the napkin and down the side of the ice cream cone.

My father said, "I don't want this shit" and he threw the ice cream in the trash. He gave us thirty more cents and told us to go back to the store and this time we better not allow any of it to drip on the napkin or down the side of the ice cream cone. As ridiculous as that sounded, my brother and I knew we had no choice but to come up with a plan. This time, my brother and I came up with a plan to wrap the ice cream cone with as many napkins as we could. Then we were going to run back to the house non-stop and that is exactly what we did. Once we purchased the ice cream we wrapped a bunch of napkins around the cone.

The clerk looked at us strangely, but we didn't care. The clerk's ass was not on the line, ours was. Gerald and I sprinted out the store. We dodged cars, people and darted across Avalon Boulevard as fast as we could. We made it home, but the ice cream still melted onto the layers of napkins that were wrapped around the ice cream cone. We were very nervous as we unwrapped layer after layer hoping at least one layer would be dry. Finally, we got to a layer of napkins that didn't have ice cream on them.

We felt confident as we went inside the house and took the ice cream to my father. I gave him the ice cream cone hoping he would be okay with how it looked. He took the ice cream cone, looked all around it and walked away. He didn't say thank you or anything. Like I said before, I truly believe my father set us up to fail and this was indeed one of those times.

He would literally put things in front of us as to basically say we were lower than he was. My siblings and I were not allowed to eat anything other than the basic food in our house. Such as chicken, meatloaf, rice, oatmeal, grits, beans and peanut butter & jelly sandwiches.

Kool-Aid was a treat at our house because water was all we could usually drink. My father, however, ate a variety of great food such as steaks, shrimp, ice cream, cookies, cakes and pies.

My mother and sisters often had to prepare two meals at the same time.

One meal was for my father and the other meal was for everyone else.

The only time we were able to eat anything other than our basic food was at breakfast on Saturdays or when guests brought food from their house. Being deprived of certain food as a child naturally made me want to know what was so good about all the stuff my father wouldn't allow us to have.

On some nights, I would steal a can of fruit cocktails from the kitchen cabinet. Once I knew I could get away with stealing the food I wasn't supposed to have, I wanted to do it more and more. Gerald was scared that I was stealing the canned fruits and bringing it back to the room to eat. He threatened to tell my father if I didn't stop. Of course I didn't stop stealing the food. Instead, I hide it from my brother instead because deep down I really believed he would tell my father.

I wasn't the only one that wanted more than what my father was giving us. He seemed to flash things in all of our faces and dare us to touch it. This man absolutely was not going to share anything with his children regardless of what it was. One day Gerald and I were in our room and my father called us into the living room.

I didn't know why, I just figured it was to look for something or maybe Gerald and I did something wrong.

He never called us for anything good. When we got to the living room, I noticed my sisters were already in there looking very afraid.

All of my sisters were there except Sharon, who was in the room and my mother who was at work.

Apparently someone took some money out of my father's pants pocket while he was in the shower. I thought no – way, who could be so bold? I just knew my father was trying to trick us. He asked all of us if we had gone into his pants pocket and taken his money.

We all replied that we hadn't. My father, determined to find the truth told all of us to form a single line. He said, "I am going to whip y'all asses over and over till one of y'all tell me who stole the money out of my pocket".

The first person he whipped was Cathy. When he got done whipping her, he asked her who stole his money out of his pants pocket. She said she didn't know and he told her to get to the end of the line.

My heart pounded rapidly as I stood in disbelief. This man was going to whip us repeatedly until someone confessed to stealing his money. By this time, we all had gotten whipped at least three times. Everyone was crying and looking at each other. It was like we wanted to say whoever stole the money, please say something. I wasn't too sure anyone of us had taken his money.

I just felt my father was starting to make things up to beat us for absolutely no reason at all. I couldn't believe this was happening and wondered where my father got his strength or the energy to beat all of us at the same time in rotation.

My father said, "I am going to give y'all one more chance to tell me the truth, go in the room and talk it over and if you don't tell me I am going to start whipping y'all again".

We all went into the first room that belonged to the girls. While we were in there, everyone suggested that it would be best for me to admit that I did it because he wouldn't be too hard on me. How is that possible I thought to myself? I am the main person he does not like.

They all somehow made me feel it would be worse on them because they were older. Where they got that idea from I had no clue, but I fell for it. We all went back into the living room and my father said, "So are y'all ready to tell me who stole the money out of my pocket?" There was a slight hesitation on my part. I looked at everyone and then I said, "I did".

My father yelled very loudly and said, "Who told you to say that?" My father was very close to my face and he was practically foaming at the mouth. I was so scared that I forgot the plan. I pointed to my siblings and I said, "They did". My father said, "Get your ass back in line". He started whipping us all over again.

Everyone was crying and to see my siblings get beat was just as bad as when I was getting beat. While one of us was getting beat by my father, we cried in line as we waited for our turn again. After a few more rotations, my oldest sister Cathy admitted that she was the one who stole the money.

My father said, "I knew all along it was you. I just wanted to see if you were going to tell the truth". My father told her that he had actually set her up because this wasn't the first time money was stolen from him.

He said he knew someone had stolen his money because he had counted it before he showered and again after he was done showering. I didn't understand why he would whip all of us if he knew who took the money all along. My father sent everyone but Cathy to his or her room.

We all limped down the hall of death, crying and holding the areas that hurt the worse. Cathy was still in the living room with my father. Needless to say, he had whipped her again for stealing his money. I knew it!! I knew he would set us up sometimes and this definitely proves it.

MATERIALISTIC

It was fall and school was about to start and I would be attending the 7th grade. On one hand I was excited because I was going to be away from this house, especially considering the kind of summer that I had. On the other hand, I was nervous about attending a bigger school. I knew school was about to get harder and that meant frequent altercations with my father.

I was going to make a great effort to get it right this time. I didn't have a tutor, or anyone to help me if I had any questions with my schoolwork, but I really was going to find some way. New school clothes and shoes were needed for the new school year. When it came to buying shoes my father actually shopped at Clark Drugs Store. The same place he would send us to buy his ice cream.

I knew I would be teased again because every kid knew what the Drugstore shoes looked like.

The market for rubber had to have been very cheap in those days because they put so much rubber on the shoes than they did fabric.

The kids would call them "bubble yums", naming them after the thick Bubble Yum chewing gum.

To be honest initially I liked the shoes. I thought every pair of new shoes looked great simply because they were new. I remember whenever my brother and I got new shoes, for some reason, we thought we were extra fast and would challenge each other to a race.

It wasn't until I went to school and all of the kids laughed at me for wearing what I found out to be cheap shoes. Kids can definitely be cruel and I learned this first hand. It was no use telling my father that I was being teased for wearing cheap shoes to school because he was going to buy the same shoes regardless.

My father would never wear shoes purchased from a Drugstore. He only wore the finest shoes such as Stacy Adams. How is it that my parents worked, had a fancy car and lived in a house that looked better than any house in the neighborhood and yet the kids looked like their parents were on welfare?

My mother never dressed better than her children. She wasn't as flashy as my father and if given the choice I think she would rather spend her money on her children before she spent it on herself.

Unfortunately, my mother didn't have a choice in how to spend the money she earned. My father handled all of the money in our family and when my mom got paid her money went straight to him. My father was not only thrifty when he bought our shoes but also when he bought our clothes.

He spent the least amount of money he could possibly spend on us and it showed. Levis was the top brand of jeans, but my father bought me these jeans called "tough-skins". I didn't feel too bad about wearing "tough skins" because just about every kid in school wore them.

Those jeans were popular among parents because they had patches on the inside of the pants where the knee bends. The patches meant they would sustain more wear and tear and last a long time. Lasting a long time was right up my father's alley. As it meant he would spend less money on us and more money on himself.

NEW SCHOOL

The year was 1977 and I would be turning 12 in three months. I was starting my first year of junior high school at Vanguard Jr. High. It was close to where we lived and located in the opposite direction of my previous elementary school.

The first day of school had finally come and it was a major step up from elementary. In elementary school, I was in one class for eight hours but in junior high I would attend six different classes at an hour at a time.

Gerald had already attended Vanguard two years prior to me coming there and was in his last year as a 9th grader. I was hoping he would make the transition a lot easier for me. Vanguard was much bigger than Mark Twain and it seemed like there was more open space on the school campus.

Vanguard had large grassy areas. They also had tennis courts, basketball courts and even a football and baseball field. It was going to take some time to get use to having six different classes, but I looked forward to it.

Art has always been my favorite thing to do because I had nothing else to do while sitting in my room except to draw.

So I was elated when I found out I had a drawing class. My art teacher's name was Mr. Dallas and he was a stern teacher who never cracked a smile. He looked a lot like Dr. Martin Luther King Jr. He was one of the teachers that believed in corporal punishment inside and outside of the classroom. That being said, the school required parents to sign a letter at the beginning of the school year, granting Mr. Dallas permission to swat us if we got out of line.

Of course, you know my father didn't have an issue with signing the form. I found out that a lot of the parents didn't give the school permission. Unfortunately, I was on the end of a few of his punishments.

I remember my very first paddling all too well. I was talking to a classmate and I had already been warned by Mr. Dallas to do my work and to stop talking.

I thought I would be smart and whisper when he wasn't looking but little did I know he didn't have to look. It was like he had eyes in the back of his head.

As he stood in front of the chalkboard, with his back to the class, Mr. Dallas called me up front without turning around. My first thought was how did he know that it was me who was talking.

I got up from my desk and as I was walking, I could see everyone looking at me as I made my way to the front of the class.

Mr. Dallas reminded me that he had already told me to stop talking and that I wasn't listening and for that reason he wanted me to follow him.

He led me to a back room where he kept his art supplies. In the corner of the room, he had a small desk and on top of the desk was a huge paddle.

The paddle was wide and had tape wrapped tightly around the handle. The part of the paddle that connected with your bottom had holes drilled into it. I don't know if this was designed to make it hurt worse or for intimidation.

He grabbed the paddle and told me to lean over the desk. I was used to getting beatings, but swats were new to me so I didn't know what to expect. As I leaned over the desk, I was nervous but ready to take my punishment.

Mr. Dallas told me to look away and as soon as I did he immediately swatted me as hard as he could. That first swat left me breathless. It was hard and stung like crazy. I received at least three more swats that were painful, but not as bad as the extension cord beatings I received at home.

The initial swat did hurt, but that was because I didn't know what to expect. After about the third swat, I looked back to see if Mr. Dallas was done and when I did he had a confused look on his face.

I guess most kids would have cried on the first swat and he looked surprised that I hadn't.

He gave me another swat and I realized he was not going to stop until he made me cry. So when he swatted me again I pretended to cry and then he stopped. I got six swats in all and not a tear came out of either eye.

It really didn't hurt. I had a feeling Mr. Dallas wanted the rest of the class to hear me being swatted. He wanted them to know the consequences of getting out of line. Unfortunately, I was the wrong student to make an example out of. Mr. Dallas escorted me out of the back room and into the classroom.

As I walked back to my desk, the entire classroom was looking to see if I was laughing or crying. I wasn't doing either one to be honest. I walked back to my desk with a straight face.

THE BIG FIGHT

School had only been in for two weeks and I didn't waste any time getting into my first fight. I didn't intend to get into a fight, but I guess someone had a lot more anger they needed to release than I did.

It happened in my fifth period math class. Mrs. Sheiks was a no nonsense teacher. She was definitely not there to make friends or to be liked by anyone. She was 5'6" with a thin build and she wore reading glasses that always seemed to rest at the tip of her nose.

On the first day of school, Mrs. Sheiks had assigned seats for each of her students. She insisted that we were to be in our assigned seats before the school bell would ring. On this day, I was running late to class and quickly rushed to my seat. When I got there, I noticed a student was sitting there. Since school had only been in for a couple of weeks, some of us had problems remembering our assigned seats so I thought nothing of it.

The student that was sitting in my seat was a kid I knew from the neighborhood. We didn't hangout, but we knew of each other.

His nickname was "Tank" but his real name was Timothy Smith. Tank had way more issues than I did.

He was always in trouble whether he was at home or school. Tank had dark skin and short nappy hair that always looked dirty. He basically walked around with a frown on his face and both fists balled up.

When I asked him if he would get up, Tank responded, "I don't see your name on this desk." I told him he was sitting at the desk Mrs. Sheiks assigned to me when school started. I told him to move and he told me to make him move.

Being the hotheaded boy that I was, I hit Tank on the side of his face and kept hitting him. Tank jumped up and grabbed me by my waist with his head down pushing me towards the wall. I continued to hit him hard on the side of his face and on the top of his head, but he would not let go of my waist. I continued to pound and pound, but Tank was not feeling a thing because he wouldn't let go.

I didn't realize that I had injured my right hand when I was hitting Tank's hard head until the fight was broken up. After the fight, I grabbed my right hand in pain. I looked at it and saw that my right hand had ballooned. Mrs. Sheiks sent both Tank and I to the office where our parents were called. I just knew I was doomed because the only parent I had at home was my father.

My mother was at work during the day and my father was working the swing shift, so he was home during school hours.

I sat in the principal's office waiting for my father to come pick me up. The only thought in my head was the beating I was about to receive. Tank was on the other side of the office with a smile on his face looking up at the ceiling. He knew he was not going to get in trouble because this was normal behavior for him.

My father had arrived and I saw the anger in his face. The school staff had no idea of the kind of man they had called. They also didn't know what he was going to do to me. The principal told my father what had happened in Mrs. Sheik's class. The only words that came out of my father's mouth were, "Come on".

I walked out of the office behind my father to the parking lot. I noticed he had driven his new Riviera to pick me up. I was a little excited about riding in his new car for the first time, but that was short-lived.

We got into his car and before I could buckle up my seat belt my father looked at me and told me he was going to beat my ass. My hand had gotten worse before my father arrived. So he took me to the hospital to see if it was broken.

On the way to the hospital my father said, "What the fuck are you doing fighting?" Before I could say a word, he took his right hand off the steering wheel and backhanded me right in my eye. I quickly held my left eye with my hands. I was dazed and crying. For a split second, a thought came across my mind to jump out of the car while it was still moving.

I would have been better off if the school had called a stranger to pick me up. This man never showed me any compassion, love or sympathy. Here I am with a hand as big as my head, already in pain and he hits me. I was getting fed up with his abuse and the way that he treated me.

He started yelling and ranting about school just starting and that I was already fighting. After cursing at me and hitting me, he had the nerve to ask me what happened?

When I told him what happened he said, "You should have told the teacher instead of taking matters into your own hands. If you want someone to fight then fight me, I just hit you now fight me". He knew I would not hit him but deep down inside I wanted to. I wanted to grab the steering wheel and hurt both of us.

Finally, we made it to the hospital. My father took me to the emergency room to have them look at my hand. I thought they would ask me about my face too. It felt like I had a black eye or a knot somewhere on my face from what my father had just done in the car. Either I didn't have a knot or they didn't see it because they didn't say anything.

After finding out my hand was not broken or fractured they bandaged my hand and told my father to make sure to ice it when I got home. My father was still angry when we left the hospital and you could tell by how fast he was driving home. I knew when we got home my father was going to tear into my behind.

He didn't say a word to me the whole time we were in the car.

When we got home, he went straight to the back room. He returned with an extension cord wrapped in his hand and made his way directly towards me. He did not care one bit about my swollen hand or that the doctor advised him to put ice on it.

At this point, nothing mattered. My father just wailed away on my behind and used every force he could muster. We danced around the living room for a little while with me leading as I tried to run away from the extension cord. On some occasions, he would hit my swollen hand with the cord and I would literally stop breathing.

After whipping me, my father gave me a lot of chores to do. He told me if I wasn't at school where I should be then I wouldn't enjoy being at home. While I was doing my chores, I didn't have any emotions.

It was like being a robot. My father never took the time to talk to me. Discussing any of my mistakes was not his way of teaching me. I couldn't believe how quick he was to beat me. Just like when he hit me first then asked me what happened. This was my father's style. He never warned me or told me what mistakes I made and how to make better decisions. Every mistake I seemed to make was followed with a beating. I knew he would be mad that I was fighting at school, but I didn't expect to get beat with an extension cord for it. I was suspended from school for a day, but I couldn't go back to school until the swelling went down in my right hand.

The doctor's request that I ice my hand was not followed. There was no medical attention administered at all. When my mother returned home from work, she asked me what happened and I told her the story.

She looked at it, but there was nothing she could do. She just told me the swelling would go down in a couple of days. I knew she couldn't be caught doing anything to help me so I took her words as comfort.

For the next few days, I was out of school and my father had me working like a dog. Whatever came to his mind is what I had to do and all with one hand. In fact, he got creative on me at times. He had me working inside and outside the house everyday from eight in the morning until four in the afternoon.

One afternoon while I was cleaning the kitchen there was a knock at the door. My father was in the living room sitting on the couch. He got up and answered it. My father said, "Yeah". It was Tank at the door. Tank said, "Hi Mr. Thompson, my name is Timothy Smith, I live around the corner and I am the one that got into a fight with your son Michael. I just wanted to apologize to Michael and to you sir because it was my fault for starting a fight.

I was sitting in his seat and I was just mad that day". My father just stood there listening. I stopped washing the dishes so I could hear the conversation. My father said, "Ok, well I appreciate you apologizing and explaining, but Michael can't have any company".

Tank said, "Ok sir but I brought him these cookies, can you give these to him and tell him that I apologized?" My father said, "Ok". Tank said, "Have a nice day sir". My father closed the door and walked into the kitchen and put the cookies on the counter near me. He knew I heard the conversation and clearly Tank just told him it was not my fault.

My father either hated to be wrong or just didn't have it in him to apologize. As I was washing dishes I was thinking, here is a kid that was not related to me, nor owed me anything and he had the decency to admit when he was wrong and apologized. Now my father hit me in the car, beat me with an extension cord and couldn't utter one word of an apology to his own son.

That day I gained so much respect for Tank. Not only for his apology but also for his taste in cookies. He brought me my favorite cookies of all, "Swiss Cookies".

ACTING OUT

A few months had passed and my birthday came around. It was November the 15th and I had turned 12 years old. No one in the house had acknowledged my birthday. There were no cards, no cake and not even a word.

Come to think of it no one has ever acknowledged anyone's birthday in that house. It was always just another day. The only reason I actually remembered my birthday is because I had to write it down at school earlier. This was definitely one of those times where I knew something just wasn't right.

I went ahead as usual and treated the day as if it was just another day. My sisters were getting older and some of them had graduated from high school. Cathy and Tonya were having many issues with my father. He was not just this way with me but with all of us. Well everyone except Sharon of course.

Cathy and Tonya ended up running away from home and I wasn't sure why they left. My father eventually found them and brought them back home. Only to have them runaway again only this time for good.

Left behind in the house was Rhonda, Diane, Gerald, Sharon and I. So much stuff was happening at home that I could no longer keep it inside. Of course around my father I had no choice, but when I was at school it was different. I began to act out a lot more and I found myself fighting before school, during school and after school.

I fought just about every day after school and mostly with the same kid. His name was Kurt. Kurt wasn't a big kid. He was slim, 5'1" with a dark complexion and one of those kids that thought he was the coolest that ever walked the earth.

I didn't think I was the coolest, but I certainly thought I was the toughest. I knew Kurt from when we attended Mark Twain Elementary School, but Kurt wasn't a fighter back then. Maybe he was afraid of William, the kid that I fought almost every day. It seemed like Kurt was trying to establish himself at Vanguard.

One morning on the way to school Kurt and I happened to be walking through the teacher's parking lot. I don't know what happened to Kurt that morning, but he looked at me with a mean scowl on his face. I thought he was mad dogging me so I gave it right back. Words were exchanged and before I knew it we were face to face.

One of the kids put an Afro pick on my shoulder and told Kurt to knock it off. There was this saying that if an item was placed on someone's shoulder while squaring off and the other person knocked it off, it meant some type of disrespect.

So Kurt knocked the Afro pick off my shoulder and the fight began. I gave Kurt a hard shove and he shoved me right back. The shoving match went back and forth for a minute with neither of us throwing any blows.

A bunch of kids surrounded us waiting for it to go down. One of the kids that surrounded us was older than we were by two years. His name was Steve.

He was my neighbor from across the street. Steve told me to handle Kurt or he was going to handle me. I took what Steve said as a vote of confidence and I took the first swing. Kurt and I were in full combat until teachers rushed in and broke it up.

I still don't know why we fought, but that fight was the beginning of many fights to come. I can't count how many fights we had, but I can say that I didn't lose any of them. From that day on, I knew I was not going to take any mess from anyone at that school.

I felt aggressive and on edge all the time. I may have accepted beatings and punishment at home, but I wanted to make sure it wouldn't happen anywhere else. The fights that Kurt and I had sent messages to the other kids at school. I had no problems from anyone from that point on.

It was my way of letting out all my frustration on someone and since it couldn't be done at home it had to be done somewhere. I was very respectful to my elders but when a kid got out of line with me I did not hesitate to put him in his place. In fact, I welcomed it.

EASTER SPECIAL

I remember one Easter my father decided he was going to dress us up and take us to church with him. Easter was the only time we went to church. We used to go to church all the time before we moved to 130th Street but since we moved we just seemed to have stopped.

My father had practiced so many religions (Christianity, Muslim, Jehovah's Witness) that he was undecided on which religion he wanted to commit to. Religion wasn't something my father tried or practiced by himself, but he had everyone in the house on the same spiritual mission as he was on.

At this particular time, he was practicing Christianity and although he didn't attend church regularly he definitely made sure we all went on Easter. Going to church on Easter Sunday was for my father more than it was for us. He wanted to doll up his kids in fancy suits, dresses and hard shiny shoes. I guess we were an extension of him. Easter was the only day my father made sure we were suited and booted. I didn't mind getting dressed up because I thought it was the only time I'd looked decent.

Any other time I had on tough skin jeans and a T-shirt and they both had holes in them. That Easter we went to church, came home, changed clothes and had a huge dinner with many guests. After the guests had gone home, it was back to normality. We had to clean up and get ready for school the next day.

The following Monday morning I got dressed for school. I ate breakfast and was ready to go. I grabbed my books, walked to the living room and told my father goodbye. As I was headed out the door, he stopped me and asked me why I didn't have on the Easter shoes he bought for me. Puzzled, I responded that I thought the Easter shoes were only for church.

Now I knew darn well it didn't matter what occasion it was, I just didn't want to wear those shoes and certainly not to school. My father told me to go back to my room and put on the Easter shoes. I couldn't believe that he was actually going to make me wear those shoes to school.

I do not recall him telling anyone else to wear his or her Easter shoes. He said he didn't pay for the shoes so I could wear them once a year and then he told me I was to wear the shoes every day to school until they were worn out.

I was upset. He didn't care that I was going to be the laughing stock of the school. It made no sense to me to wear those shoes to school. I put those horrible shoes on with my eyes full of tears. These shoes didn't even go with what I had on.

I had on green tough skin jeans, a black t-shirt and now some brown dress shoes. I didn't know what to do or what to think. I grabbed my books, told my father bye and was off to school. While I was walking to school, I prayed that I wasn't going to be the only kid with Easter shoes on.

The sound of my shoes making a galloping noise was enough for me to be embarrassed to wear them. While I was walking I tried my best to walk on the grass so the kids wouldn't hear me, but unfortunately there wasn't that much grass along the way to school.

When I got to school not a single sole had on Easter shoes but me. As I walked in the hallways, the sound of my shoes was even louder. Each step echoed in the hallways. Kids were looking down at my shoes and I felt completely humiliated. I may not have heard them talking about me, but I knew they were. I wanted to ditch school so bad.

I made it through the day but not without a few jokes and snickering from the other kids. I really hope I didn't have to wear those shoes the next day, but if I did have to wear them, I had to think of a plan and quick. A great idea came to mind. I was going to wear the shoes out of the house and stash them in a nearby alley.

Then after school I would change back into my Easter shoes. Later that night when I showed my father my clothes he reminded me not to forget that I was wearing my Easter shoes to school until they were worn out. It was something I anticipated my father saying.

I felt better that I already had a plan. The next morning when I got ready for school I had my Easter shoes on and I told my father goodbye and went out the door.

Before I was forced to wear these shoes, I would always wear my knock off Chuck Taylors. I needed them for gym class. So now I had to carry my sneakers with me because I didn't have a bag to put them in.

When I was walking through the alley, I found a place to tuck my shoes away. I looked around carefully to make sure no one saw where I put them and then I changed into my sneakers. This worked for a few days until one day I hid the shoes under some wood and when I came back from school the shoes were not there.

In fact, the pile of wood was completely gone. I was terrified. My first thought was maybe I put them somewhere else. I looked around the whole alley and then it dawned on me that there was no trash in the alley at all.

What I didn't know is that the street sweeper came and cleared away all the debris in the alley. Instantly, I got a real sickening feeling in my stomach. I felt like vomiting. I didn't know how I was going to explain this to my father. I was pissed at myself for being so stupid.

I should have just worn the shoes and dealt with the teasing at school. I knew I was going to get beat by my father. Every step I took was like walking down the street with solid iron balls on my ankles.

As people drove by I wished I were going away with them. I saw kids going home happy and hurrying to get home. I even saw a cop car passing and I thought of flagging them down. I was barely walking and calling myself stupid repeatedly under my breath.

I knew my father would notice I didn't have my Easter shoes on the minute I walked through the front door. Something inside of me told me not to go home at all, to just run away and never come back. I hadn't run away before because I was too afraid and I had nowhere to go. Now was no different.

I decided to go home and face the music. When I got to the front door of our house, I hesitated. The visual I had of my father beating me played in my head over and over again. My heart was pounding and I could hardly swallow.

I wished that Gerald was there with me, but my father didn't allow us to wait on each other. We were to come straight home. As nervous as I was I managed to turn the doorknob and open the front door and when I entered the house my father was sleeping on the couch. I walked as quietly as I could. I passed by him and hurried down the hallway of death. I was praying each step of the way that he wouldn't wake up and call me. I went into my room, closed the door and breathed a sigh of relief. For now, I had gotten away with it. I knew in the morning I would be in trouble, but I bought some time. My father eventually found out the next morning because I couldn't produce my Easter shoes.

I told him that I didn't want to wear the shoes because I was being teased at school so I hid them in the alley. I told him that when I went back to the alley the shoes were gone. My father hit the roof. The look I was given was pure evil as if I disgusted him.

He jumped up and constantly punched me in the head with his fist as I cried and tried to protect myself. I felt like I was getting beat up by someone in the streets. Then he grabbed his belt from his waistband and started whipping me with it while he yelled and screamed at me. I knew this would happen, I just had to weather the storm with no umbrella. There were times I felt I deserved a whipping and to some degree I felt this was one of them.

I made a dumb decision and one that I wish I could have taken back. I was on a punishment for a very long time. Part of my punishment was that I had to wear similar Easter shoes that my father went out and purchased again.

The Shoes were even worse than before. They were green and pointy. They made me wish I hadn't lost the other pair. I knew he bought them to be spiteful and mean, but there wasn't anything I could do. This time I wore the shoes to school until they practically dissolved.

THE BREAK

There were many times I wanted my mother to leave my father and save herself. On many occasions, I thought she would have and especially when he would beat her. I knew that a person could only take so much. I thought to myself that he was going to beat on my mother one time and she is going to leave and never come back.

One night my mother asked my father if she could go to her mother's house where they were having a get together. To my surprise my father told her that she could go.

He didn't like going over my mother's parent's house much, so he drove my mother to their house. It wasn't that far, they lived about 10 minutes away on 122nd street and Broadway. He dropped my mother off and returned home.

In all, it took no longer than fifteen minutes. A few hours later as I was cleaning the kitchen I heard the phone ring and my father answered the phone.

I couldn't hear what was being said on the other end of the phone, but I had an idea it was my mother.

It sounded as if my mother was asking my father if he could come pick her up from her parent's house. He appeared a bit agitated. He told her no and to find another way home then he hung-up the phone. About twenty minutes went by and my mother called back to let my father know that she still needed a way home.

My father yelled and said, "It's late and you need to get your ass home". He then slammed the phone down on the receiver. I knew this wasn't going to be good and I did not want to see the outcome of this argument. I just hoped that my mom would hurry and get here.

After doing the dishes, I went to my room to go to bed. It was around 9:30 p.m. The door to my bedroom was cracked open. Gerald was already in bed, but he wasn't asleep. Ten minutes later I heard the front door open and I assumed it was my mother.

In a deeply enraged tone, my father asked her who dropped her off. My mother responded that a male friend of the family drove her home. All of a sudden my father became belligerent and began cursing and yelling.

He said, "What in the fuck is wrong with you? You do not get in the car with any mother-fucking man. I don't care if you don't have a way home." My mother reminded my father that she had called him twice and he refused to come get her.

My mother also told my father that she didn't understand why he was getting upset.

She said it was getting late and she was trying to get anyone to bring her home.

My father said, "I don't give a fuck what excuse you have!" At that point, I heard a loud smacking sound as if someone had gotten slapped.

The next thing I heard was rumbling and my mother telling my father to stop. She was trying to explain how she had no choice.

I could hear hurried footsteps as if my mother was trying to run from my father. I had seen before how my mother would run around the house from the living room to the kitchen to prevent my father from hitting her.

She was crying and my father was cursing at her. By this time, Gerald and I had both gotten out of bed and were at the door trying to see but we didn't want to be seen ourselves.

So we didn't stick our heads out. We both were angry and Gerald was very upset and stated he wanted to kill my father and suggested we both do so.

It sounded like a good idea at the time and we were ready but our feet would not budge. All of a sudden, we heard more rumbling and my mother fell and cried out loud, "You broke my leg, you broke my leg Jack, you broke my leg". My heart sank and quietly I began to cry.

I didn't know what to do, but I was so emotionally crushed. I had seen black eyes and swollen lips on my mother many times.

She would always tell people it was an accident from falling or hitting her eye on the door. We would just look at her and wished she would tell the truth, but we never understood why she wouldn't.

I don't think the people she explained this to believed any of her explanations either, but they weren't going to call her on it. Helpless as kids could be, Gerald and I just stayed by the door and cried. I'm not sure if the girls heard what was happening. I am sure they did because their room was closer to the living room where my parents were. I wondered what was going through their minds

My father said, "Get up there's nothing wrong with you". My mother said, "Yes it is and I can't move it". My father yelled from the living room for Gerald and I. We went into the living room as fast as we could and acted as if we had just woken up. I saw my mother sitting on the floor between the kitchen and living room crying with my father kneeling down next to her.

He told us to go in the shed and get the crutches. Gerald and I ran fast as we could to the shed to get the crutches. We were digging around in the shed looking for the crutches while trying to keep our emotions inside. By the time we returned to the house my father had helped my mother to the couch and was tending to her.

We gave him the crutches and I looked at my mom to see if she was ok. She was still crying and it took all of my strength to keep from doing the same. He told us to go back to bed and we did. Fuming and hurt I climbed into my bed and cried.

I never saw my mother like this and I thought my father had gone too far. I was thinking of all kinds of ways to kill my father, but every idea I thought of wasn't good enough.

I wanted to fall asleep fast because I couldn't take hearing my mother cry any longer. I was hoping this was a bad dream.

The next morning I realized that this was no dream but a living nightmare. My mother was in her bed with her leg in a cast and it was elevated on pillows.

I guess my father must have taken her to the hospital when we went to sleep. No one asked her anything about her leg. We all heard what happened and just pretended that nothing did.

The girls stepped up in the house and took over most of my mom's duties. They cooked, cleaned and made sure dinner was ready for my father and us. We helped my mother out around the house and got things for her when she needed them. Basically, the same thing we did for my father when he hurt his leg only this time we really wanted to help.

It was hard to look my father in the eyes after that night. When I did look at him, all I saw was a monster. Every time I was in the same room with him I became angry and disgusted. Thoughts of killing my father were still in the front of my mind. So was running far away.

AFTER SCHOOL SPECIAL

My father decided to convert our two-car garage into a man cave. The first thing he did was bolt down the garage door so that it could no longer be raised. He had us help him put white and brown wall paneling all around the walls in the garage.

I hated working alongside my father. Everything we did was wrong in his eyes and with the constant yelling and screaming we were nervous the whole time. It was something I expected, but nothing I could get use to. Either we were not fast enough, or not good enough for whatever he needed us to do.

After installing the paneling on the garage walls, he then installed a wall heater. He later installed a ceiling using 12x12 tiles, built a custom bar, added mirrors and lastly carpet. My father's man cave was officially established. It took about two weeks for this project. Not to mention a few beatings along the way. The garage really turned out nice. I know this was not a place for any of his kids, but I sure hoped he liked it enough to never come out.

My father spent most of his days in the garage when he was not working or yelling at us.

I kind of liked the idea because it kept him out of the house and we were able to spend more time watching T.V. with my mother.

The shows that my mother liked watching we liked as well. I don't know what my father did while he was in the garage because the door was usually closed. I knew he played music a lot because I could hear it through the walls. The less I saw my father, the better things were. At least that's what I thought would be the case.

I was 14 years old and in the 9th grade. School became difficult for me because it was hard for me to stay focused. My thoughts always seemed to be scrambled and somewhere other than where they should have been. When I was at school, I was constantly thinking about home.

Things like, if I had done my chores or thinking about the beating I was promised the next day because I forgot to do something. I also thought a lot about watching my mother and siblings get beat, cursed and mistreated. I was no longer able to block out things that were happening at home. I was so depressed and lost. Every day that I went to school my mind was literally blank.

I was having constant thoughts of life at home and I couldn't think of anything else. Every day I knew it was always going to be something that my father would find to give him a reason to beat me.

Consequently, education was not important to me. Deep down I enjoyed school and loved the idea of learning, but learning was starting to be so difficult.

Even reading was becoming difficult and I really enjoyed it. Whenever I was doing work in school or got homework it all seemed foreign. There was so much negative distraction from home, no motivation to do well in school and the situation didn't seem like it was going to change. I often thought, what was the purpose for learning if my life was going to be like this?

All of my life it seemed as if every day I had been beat talked down too and hated. I was torn, I didn't want to stay in school and I didn't want to go home either.

I pretended to be happy when the school bell rang to go home just like the other kids. The difference is they were really happy to go home and I was dreading it.

One day when I got home from school my father had something waiting on me that I didn't foresee. Normally while taking that dreadful walk home my thoughts were, did I forget to take out the trash, did I wash the dishes right or did I show him my clothes?

I had no idea when I got home my father would have a chalkboard in the garage.

My father approached me as soon as I entered the house and said, "Put your books down, change your clothes and come into the garage." When I went into the garage, the chalkboard had math problems on it waiting for me. He said, "I want you to grab the chalk and do those math problems". Out of all the math problems he could have given me, he started me out on fractions.

Now basic math I already knew how to do but now he wanted me to learn fractions. I looked at it and I knew this was going to be a long night.

I told him I never did these before. He came to the board and showed me how to do one of them and then told me to do the next one. Even though he just showed me how to solve the problem my mind was not there. I was already thinking ahead of what was about to happen once he realized I couldn't solve the problem.

I wanted to put the chalk down and just let him beat the hell out of me. I tried my best to follow his instructions, but I honestly couldn't get it. My mind was literally blank.

At the time all I could think of was my father, the stick and what always came next. He could have asked me how to spell my name and I doubt I would have spelled it right. I wanted to snap out of the trance or state of mind I was in and do what he told me to do.

For some reason I couldn't. I had no idea what was going on with me. My father was a very impatient man and got angry when he thought he explained something simple.

Whenever I didn't get what he was saying he would yell and curse at me. That would cause me to become completely defensive. I just stood there blindly writing numbers on the chalkboard pretending I knew the answer but all along I was anticipating a striking blow. It was coming, when exactly I didn't know but I knew it was coming.

With no warning my father whacked me with the pointer stick and yelled and cursed. He swung the pointer at me again this time breaking it across my back.

I didn't see when the blows were coming because my back was to him but I braced for the worse. He then hit me on the side of my face with what felt like a closed fist. I covered my face and tried to protect myself as he continued to yell and hit me. He went to the board to explain the problem again but I didn't hear a word he said because while he was yelling I was crying. In an hour's time I got yelled at, cursed at and hit while trying to do one equation.

My father was determined to get me to complete the equation. Even though I really wanted to, I continued to draw a blank.

At this point I was hoping that my mom or someone would come through the door and stop my father's abuse but at the same time I knew it was wishful thinking. I just wanted it to stop. Please God, make him stop is what I would repeatedly say in my head.

This treatment that my father constantly gave me day in and day out was debilitating.

After four hours of being beat with his hands and yelled at, I was finally able to do that one equation.

Of course he showed me over and over. I guess he felt we had a break through and he ended the lessons. I am not sure how I got the answer correct but I was so glad it was over. Day after day I had after school sessions in the man cave with my father.

He continued to cram problem after problem into my head. I had already dreaded coming home prior to all the lessons and this didn't make it any better.

He eventually moved the chalkboard into the living room. I have no idea why. I guess I was interfering with the privacy he had in the garage. The way my father taught was not working for me. I didn't understand the math problems at all. I really wanted to learn how to do the fractions so the torture would stop. Even after the beatings and solving the problems, I never had a clue how I did it. My father was happy when I did solve the problem because I think it gave him a sense of validation. Validation for beating me like he did and to show my mother and siblings his method worked.

One day after school I was walking home and I turned the corner to my house and to my surprise I saw my brother Cedric in the driveway. I was shocked to see that he was home from the Army.

I was so happy to see him that I ran up to him, wrapped my arms around him and said, "Hey Cedric!" Cedric responded with a hug and a smile. He looked taller and a little stronger but still thin.

Out of all us boys I was the one that had more meat on my bones but they were taller then I was. Cedric was about 6'0" tall, which was taller than my father at 5'10". I felt a sense of relief just having him there. I wanted to ask him so many questions about how things were in the Army and if he had to go to war and more. My father came outside and told me nothing had changed.

He said, "Get inside so I can teach you the math lessons". I was instantly deflated. I had not seen my older brother for such a long time and I just wanted to spend a little time with him. I went inside the house and school began. Cedric was in the garage. I guess my father let him stay in the man cave while he was visiting from the Army. I think maybe that was why my father moved the chalkboard from the garage to the living room.

My mother was in the kitchen getting dinner together and my siblings were at the dining room table doing their homework.

I changed clothes and came back into the living room. He gave me the piece of chalk and told me to solve the problems. My father had written about ten math problems on the board prior to me getting there. I did the first four problems right and got stuck on the fifth one. This problem seemed to be a little different than the others and I just couldn't get it.

As I stood there pondering the problem my father tried to help me along but I couldn't get this one. I knew this was not a problem I had seen before, but I guess he was introducing me to a new one. My father began to raise his voice in anger and curse me. I became nervous, scared and blanked out even more. I knew he was going to lose it completely and it was just a matter of time.

He snatched the chalk out my hands and yelled at me. He wrote down an example on the board so I can see what he wanted me to do, but I still was not getting it.

Fear took over again. I was very familiar with this scenario. I knew the hit was going to happen at any time, either with his new stick or his fists.

My father said, "I just showed you how to do the fucking problem so what are you waiting for?" As he was flailing his hands, I jumped because I thought he was going to strike me. I was a nervous wreck and my legs felt like wet noodles. My father yelled, "Don't sit there and hold the damn chalk do the problem damn it." I just froze as tears streamed down my face and my mind went blank. He hit me with a wooden pointer as hard as he could across my back.

The pain was so great I began to cry. I tried to focus and I raised my hand to the chalkboard but nothing was there. The math problems were simple for my father but new to me. He didn't realize that I needed him to have more patience. He also didn't realize I couldn't be in learning mode because he was yelling, cursing and hitting me. I wanted to drop that chalk and cry at the chalkboard. I was overwhelmed with varied emotions simultaneously.

My father kept yelling and he hit me with the pointer again. As I was crying I looked at him puzzled because I didn't know what he wanted under the circumstances. I looked at the chalkboard and then back at him. I had a lot of thoughts running through my head, but none of them were related to math.

Did he see that I wasn't learning the way he was teaching me? Did he think to break the problem down?

No, instead he continued to strike me with a wooden pointer. I saw him in my peripheral vision about to hit me with the stick again and I raised my hand to pretend to write something on the chalkboard just to stall for a second.

Suddenly, Cedric came out of the garage and said, "Why don't you leave him alone you see he don't know the answer". I began to cry out loud. I couldn't hold it in anymore and I needed someone to know the abuse I was suffering. To have someone for the first time in my life step in while I was getting beat and say something on my behalf made me extremely emotional.

It was a prayer answered and I'm glad the person that stepped up was my brother Cedric. The feelings that I felt were indescribable. I wanted to run, scream and hide behind my brother.

The shocked look on my father's face was priceless. He was speechless and just stood in place staring at Cedric. He wasn't the only person with a shocked look on their face. My mother and siblings all seemed to freeze. There was my brother standing tall, fierce and standing up to my father for his little brother.

My father yelled to Cedric, "What in the hell are you talking about? He knows the answer to this problem." My brother said, "Well that's not what I'm hearing." You keep hitting him with this stick even though you see he doesn't know the answer."

Cedric said, "Maybe that is why he can't do it because he is scared he might get hit."

My father told my brother that he has taught me the math problem many times before and I understood them.

Then my father said, "Who the fuck are you to tell me what to do?" He told my brother he better go back in the garage and mind his business. My father and Cedric went back and forth with their loud discussion. I just knew my father would go after my brother, but that never happened.

Even my mother came into the living room thinking she might have to get in between them. My brother said, "That's not how you teach someone. You can't learn that way." My father said, "I must know what I am doing look at you. Look how you turned out." My brother said, "It's not because of you".

Then my father asked, "So are you telling me that you aren't who you are because of how I raised you?" My mother stepped in and said, "Okay Jack you are the one that asked him that question if he answers the way he wants to, are you going to get mad?"

My father responded that he wasn't going to get mad but that he wanted to know what Cedric thought. My brother told my father that he had nothing to do with the kind of man he turned out to be. That he had become who he was on his own. The living room grew quiet. I stood nervously by the chalkboard sniffing, shaking and afraid to see what would happen next.

Afraid of what my father would do to me next. My father hastily walked out the room and down the hallway to his bedroom.

I looked at my brother and wanted desperately to hug him, but he walked back into the garage before I could do so. My mother told me to go to the kitchen table and do my homework.

I can't believe a part of me was actually feeling sorry for my father. This man was basically caning me without remorse and I felt sorry for him. I always felt my father was mean, but I also knew my father was a smart, strong and talented man. Those are the traits I admired about him.

If only I could inherit just his good traits, I could be a good person. I wasn't sure what was next but for now I appreciated my brother for standing up to my father.

My brother didn't stay in the garage that day because of the tension between him and my father. It became apparent that someone had to go and unfortunately, it wasn't my father.

My brother's courage didn't deter my father from practicing the very same harsh teaching tactics with me.

The next day at the chalkboard my father was just as determined as ever to get me to learn what he wanted me to learn.

GOOD GLIMPSE

It was rare that my father treated us well. I remember one of the good things my father did with us was taking us to the Pike in Long Beach. The Pike had cool games and carnival rides and was an overall good place for families to have fun.

My father took us to the Pike once every three or four months. He would also take us to the drive-in movies every blue moon. Of course, he would only take us in the station wagon and not in his new car. Whenever we went somewhere my father never yelled at us. Times like these we were one big happy family and he was a normal family man. We never took anything he did nice for us for granted.

We appreciated his nice gestures towards us and soaked it all in because we knew this wasn't going to last too long. We became use to not expecting my father to treat us well. We adopted the idea that if it happens great and if it doesn't it was normal.

Another fun time was Christmas. I have no idea why he celebrated some holidays and not others. My father bought Christmas presents for everyone.

I remember he bought us those skates with the steel wheels. They were called "Street Kings". Street Kings rode roughly on the concrete and they were loud.

Whenever I stopped skating my legs would still be vibrating from skating on the pavement. Most of the kids in the neighborhood had gotten skates also, but they had gotten the good skates.

They were called "Roller Derby's". Roller Derby's had a much smoother ride. We weren't expecting anything from my father so we were happy with what we had gotten.

My father also would buy Gerald and I bags of plastic soldiers, cowboys and Indians and yellow Tonka Trucks.

I marveled over how durable the Tonka trucks were because they were made of steel and lasted longer than anything I've ever owned. My father bought the girls skates as well and a few dolls.

We didn't get to play with our sisters that often but when Christmas came around we would all play outside together. My mother would be in the house cooking a nice Christmas dinner.

I use to love when she would set out the walnuts and hard color candies. She would also set out apples and oranges for us. I can't recall ever hearing any arguments or witnessing any abuse by my father on Christmas. Honestly, Christmas was the best time of year because it was the only time I could remember my father doing things for us.

I always looked forward to the good things my father did because the good things he did gave me hope that my father wasn't as bad as he seemed. I made mental recording of these times and cherished them to the fullest. I would go back on them in thought until the next time my father felt normal.

ENVY

My father was exceptionally close to his older sister Edna. They had similar personalities. The only difference between my father and my aunt was that my Aunt Edna cared more about her children, put them before herself and rarely spanked her children.

My father on the other hand, put himself before his children, cared more about other people and spanked us for any reason. Auntie was a compassionate upfront woman who wasn't the type to hold her tongue. My aunt's sense of humor was hilarious and she too had a hearty laugh and laughed often.

She was a knowledgeable woman and she often told me stories or gave me valuable life lessons that I will never forget. She was a typical Gemini with two distinct personalities. She was a blast to be around but let's just say, there were a side to her you did not want to experience.

Still, it amazed me how my father and my aunt had similar personalities yet they expressed themselves differently. My aunt was fun to be around and she was a comedian in her own right.

I found myself laughing at some of the uncanny things she would say.

On the weekends, when my aunt came to our house, the first thing I heard was her loud and jovial voice. I would say to myself, "yes, auntie is here." I always felt good when she came over and wished she'd stay longer than she did.

She adored my mother and my mother adored her despite their two different personalities. My aunt was like a big sister to my mom. She would always look out for my mom when she was visiting our house.

She would fuss at my dad if he did or said anything mean to my mom or any of the kids while she was there. She was not afraid of my father because her temper was just as vicious as his. Whenever she chastised him about something he'd said or did, my father would just laugh it off. Surprisingly, my father and aunt got along well and were very close despite both of them having explosive personalities.

My mother's side of the family seemed to be close as well. They always had outings and events together and even though my mother's siblings lived in other states, they would fly into town whenever the family had a big event. My mother's side of the family was quiet, relaxed and low key. They were the exact opposite of my father's side of the family. I didn't get a chance to hang around my mother's side of the family, but my father would allow me to hang around his side of the family.

I had some exciting times whenever I went to my aunt's house.

My Aunt Edna would ask my father if I could visit her for the weekend and my father would allow me to go. I knew better than to ask my father myself because the answer would always be no simply because I was the one who was asking. So I would ask my aunt to ask my dad instead.

Things were totally different at my aunt's house. I was able to see how she interacted with her children. Something I had always wondered about. Even though she never hesitated to chastise her children when necessary you could tell she loved them. My aunt's children were not afraid of her and the house was usually filled with love and laughter.

My aunt taught her children many different things and explained to them why she wanted them to do the things she asked them to do.

The difference between my aunt's house and our house was that, in her house, her kids had a voice. If we had a voice in my father's house, it's because we were crying. My cousins didn't disrespect my aunt, but they were allowed to tell her what concerned them and what they did or didn't like.

Even the atmosphere at my aunt's house was totally different. There was no yelling, it was peaceful and my cousins had the freedom to get what they wanted from the refrigerator without asking for permission. My cousins spent a lot of time with their friends outside. They were allowed to stay out pretty late too.

I had gotten use to being inside the house when I was at home so I didn't feel the need to hang outside. Instead, I stayed in the house and talked to my Aunt Edna, Uncle Lee and my older male cousins that were there. We played Tonk, which is a card game we would play every time I visited. It was our favorite game. We played for a nickel a hand and before you knew it auntie would come with her huge jar of change and set it on the table. Sometimes we would play that game until 4:00 a.m. No arguing or beatings just laughter.

My cousins knew how well they had it but like all kids they would sometimes test the limits with my aunt. One morning while I was spending the weekend over my aunt's house, she made my cousin Derek, James and I some eggs and grits. She fixed everyone's plate and sat it in front of us. Whenever I had grits at home I always had to have sugar. So I asked my aunt if I could have some sugar for my grits.

She was surprised and said, "You eat sugar in your grits?" I said, "yes". She said, "Ok" and handed me the sugar jar. My younger cousin James saw that and told my aunt he wanted some sugar in his grits, and my aunt said, "Oh boy you never eat sugar in your grits". She told my cousin to eat his food and stop copying what Michael does. My cousin got mad and was looking as if he wanted to cry. My aunt saw him and asked him what was wrong.

In a whining voice, he said, "I want some sugar in my grits". The look on my aunt's face was so familiar.

She started cursing and said, "Boy you know damn well you don't eat sugar in your damn grits". She went to him and grabbed his plate and dumped the whole plate in the sink. My little cousin ran out the kitchen crying. Like I said Aunt Edna was sweet as pie but when rubbed the wrong way, look out. My cousin Derek and I couldn't stop laughing. That became a running joke between my cousins and I. My aunt worked hard every day.

She was a custodian for the Los Angeles Unified School District. She bought my cousins nearly everything they wanted and they sometimes complained if she bought the wrong color or the wrong type. If I could have switched places with one of my cousins, I would have in a heartbeat. My cousins knew how my father was because they spent the night once and never asked to spend another night again.

They often teased me when I came over and they had a lot of jokes about my father. We would all laugh as they impersonated him. I didn't get upset because the jokes were about how my father really was. Instead, I laughed right along with them.

I envied many of my friends and family members for the relationships they had with their parents. I envied the freedom they had and the love they seemed to get from their parents. I was beginning to see what life was like for other kids. I realized that the way our family was treated wasn't normal.

THOUGHTLESS

My father did not allow my mother to show us any type of affection whatsoever. Nor did he show us any type of affection. It's not that my mother wasn't affectionate it's just that my father didn't allow affection to be displayed in his home. Not from the parent to children or amongst ourselves. Maybe the only person that may have felt some type of affection was my little sister Sharon since she seemed like my father's favorite.

It's weird because I don't remember a hug, kiss or any terms of endearment from my parents or siblings. It just didn't exist. I didn't doubt for one minute that my mom loved me or that my siblings and I loved each other. It just seems to be an unspoken rule in our house not to express love.

I remember one day I got in trouble for forging some grades on my report card. The teacher called my father and told him what I did.

My father was furious. I knew I was wrong, but I was operating in survival mode. My report card was not good and I already knew what the end result would be. I knew I had to either forge the grades or get beat.

At that point in my life all my thoughts and actions were pre-calculated to delay the beatings whether it would be delayed for an extra hour, day or week. There were times I wish I were allowed a do-over. A time where I could tell my dad that I messed up and I just needed a clean slate. Maybe even just ask him for help.

I never had that opportunity. Instead, I always found myself a step behind. My father expected everything I did to be done right the first time or there was hell to pay. Whether I forged my grades or not, I was going to get in trouble and if I could delay the consequences I would and I did.

We were given our report cards in an unsealed envelope to take home to our parents. When I was walking home, I opened my report card and saw that my grades were bad and I knew I was going to get a beating.

I stopped walking, reached into my pocket and got out a pen to forge my grades. I changed two "F's" that I got in Math and Science into "A's". I did a great job of forging those grades thanks to the art class I took with good ole Mr. Dallas.

When I got home, I gave my father my report card and hoped he would not notice anything wrong. He looked at the report card and I stood there sweating and it wasn't even hot outside. I waited there for a few seconds as he looked over the report card then he put it down. He didn't say a word to me. He just started watching television again. I headed to my room to change my clothes.

A few days had gone by and although my report card was bad I enjoyed the days of not getting in trouble for it. My actions bought me some time and peace of mind.

When my teacher asked me about my report card, I told her that my father hadn't looked at it yet. It took me a few more days before I finally decided to give my report card to my teacher, but there was something I had overlooked. I didn't anticipate that my teacher would check to see if the parents' signature was on the report card. When my teacher checked for the signatures on my report card, she noticed that I had changed my grades.

I had no idea she had called my father and told him about what I did, so I wasn't expecting any issues when I got home. Well, when I got home from school, my father yelled and cursed at me the moment I stepped foot in the house. He told me he was going to beat my ass like he never beat it before.

I knew this would be the beating of all beatings. I knew my father wasn't going to let this slide. If I had it to do all over again, I would make the same decision and spare myself a few days before the beating. After all, I was going to get beat anyway for whatever reason it was.

In some instances, it seemed like my father liked to delay my punishments by telling me it was coming. I preferred he got it over with, but I had no say in the matter. Whatever strategy he had it was no longer having the same effect.

Nonetheless, I still wished he did it right away. It seemed like every hour on the hour I expected my father to grab the extension cord and say bring your ass in here.

I had graduated to the extension cord full-time now and the belt was no longer an option. I guess in my father's mind the belt was no longer working on me.

Consequently, if my father didn't have an extension cord nearby he would use his fists and get an extension cord immediately afterwards. Had he asked me what I preferred I would have chosen the belt.

I was doing my chores in the bathroom and like any other chore there was an art to cleaning the bathroom. Fortunately the bathroom was not as technical as the kitchen. As I was finishing up the bathroom, I could hear my father snoring on the couch. I assumed he was dead tired and I would be cool for the night. I was very familiar with him playing possum so I wasn't too excited.

I was glad, however, that I didn't have to wake him because it was Friday night and I didn't have to show him my clothes for the next day. Things were working in my favor and I thought I might make it through the night without a beating after all.

After I had finished mopping the bathroom floor, I went to my room. I knew he was capable of waking up and surprising me so I thought ahead. Just in case he was going to whip me tonight I put on an extra pair of underwear and pajamas.

I lay in my bed and attempted to go to sleep. While I was lying there, I listened for his signature movements. It was hard to do because every cough and swallow that I heard through his snoring made my stomach turn knots. I couldn't go to sleep because I was nervous.

My father always unbuckled his belt before he lay on the couch. As he tossed and turned on the couch, I could hear the sound of his belt buckle.

I had learned to listen for a combination of sounds but mainly the sounds I listened for were my father's house shoes slipping and sliding. My father stopped snoring and was sort of choking. He coughed a few more times and then I didn't hear anything else. I was waiting to hear him start snoring again but then I heard the sound of his belt buckle.

Then for some reason I heard nothing at all. I was going nuts with the covers over my head praying to God to make it through the night. My father's belt started jingling and I heard him in the kitchen running water.

I was scared to death and praying he didn't come in my room that night. Suddenly, my father's belt jingled and the sound of his house shoes was slipping and sliding down the hallway.

I knew he was headed for my room and it seemed like an eternity for him to get there. My throat had become so dry and tight from anxiety I couldn't swallow and I began crying silently.

The sound of my father's belt buckle and house shoes became louder as he got closer to my bedroom door.

My father opened my door, flicked on the lights and said, "Get your ass up." As usual in his hand was the infamous extension cord. I started crying loudly way before he even touched me. My father hit me with a few hard and powerful strokes. Even though I had on extra clothing it still hurt when he hit me.

He must have noticed I had on extra clothing because he told me to strip naked. I took off all my clothing and he said, "Oh so you think you are smart huh?"

My father started beating me while I was bare and I could have died from every strike. Every time the cord connected with my skin I felt my skin rip and burn. On my mind were two things. I prayed that God would make him stop or kill me.

This had to have been the hardest my father had ever whipped me with an extension cord. Not only that but I had no layer of clothing to help ease the pain. It became clear to me that my father was beating me with strength I had never previously experienced.

The cord made a loud crackling sound when it connected with my bare flesh. I repeatedly gasped for air as I struggled to breathe. Then I thought if I hold my breath I could make my heart stop.

I held my breath for as long as I could at one time during the beating again hoping to die. The pain from the extension cord slicing into my flesh would not allow me to escape my reality.

He beat me for what seemed like forever but in real time it was only a few minutes.

I jumped around constantly and used my hands to try to block some of the blows, but that didn't work. My father would occasionally pause from beating me to catch his own breath and would curse and yell. Then he would squeeze and bend my wrists to keep me from moving and start again. I thought to myself surely the neighbors are hearing me.

I hoped that someone called the police and at any time now they would come crashing down the door and take my father away.

When my father was done beating me, he turned off the lights and told me to get in the bed. I got in bed as fast as I could, still shaking and squirming uncontrollably. I was all cried out, no more tears left. I tried to lay in many positions but as I lay there naked I was in pain. There wasn't a spot on me he didn't touch with that extension cord.

I remember squeezing myself real hard as if I was trying to squeeze the life out of me. I moaned and groaned in frustration because I couldn't stop feeling the pain and despair. I became enraged and I believe that was my turning point where I started to hate.

I didn't only hate my father, but also life, as I knew it. I knew someone heard my cries, but no one cared. I don't remember how I fell asleep that night.

I wouldn't have been surprised if I had lost consciousness after the beating I had endured. I would have rather been dead than to wake up again in my father's house.

I wanted to die that night so I didn't have to suffer another day. As a child, I didn't know where the idea of "God" or the knowledge of prayer came from. I never knew how to make that connection, but that night as inexperienced as I was, I prayed for God.

At about 7:00 a.m. my mother knocked on the door and told us to wake up. I realized that my prayer never to wake up again wasn't answered.

As I was getting up I felt such incredible pain that I let out a loud scream and I didn't care who heard me. I could tell I startled Gerald because he looked at me in shock. Gerald was in the same room listening to the beating my father gave me last night. I'm sure the cover was over his head as he lay motionlessly.

My mother rushed into our room to find out what was wrong. I cried and told her my skin hurt. As she removed the blanket that covered me she gasped. She noticed that my father had beaten me with the extension cord while naked. The beating my father gave me caused open wounds all over my body that had stuck to my sheets as I slept. I had deep cuts in my skin that were still bleeding. The sores on my legs were bad.

The look on my mother's face was pure sadness. Tears welled up in her eyes as she listened to her child cry in pain.

My mother was getting ready to tend to me when my father came into the room and asked what the hell is going on.

My mother told him the sheet was stuck to my open wounds and my father told my mother to stop babying me and to get the hell out of the room. He said, "I told you about babying these boys." My mother ran out the room crying.

Then my father turned to me and yelled, "Get your fucking ass up now!" I was scared so I jumped up. As I got up, I screamed again because the sheet that was fitted to my mattress yanked the fresh scabs off my wounds and I began to bleed again.

I felt pure agony. As I cried aloud, I fumbled around for my clothes. My father said, "That's what you get and it's going to be worse next time, now hurry up and get dressed and go clean the fucking yard." My father had no sympathy for my condition. My father had no emotions, no concerns and no care. I could understand if he didn't want to show me any love and affection, but I never understood why he wouldn't allow my mother to show me any. In my mind, I was sure he was pure evil.

It was hard to put on my clothes without the material rubbing and scratching against my raw wounds. I cried throughout, but I didn't stop putting on my clothes. I knew I had to hurry or get this all over again. Walking was even worse because with every step I took my clothes brushed against my open wounds. My wounds were never attended to. They opened and closed throughout the day.

My brother and I finished working in the yard and were called in for breakfast. I felt like a walking zombie except I was feeling pain.

No emotions, no thoughts and no feelings. I really didn't have an appetite but my father's rule was you had to make sure everything was off your plate whether it was breakfast or dinner. After forcing the food down my mouth, I left to go to my room where I was ordered to stay as a punishment. I was reading a book and trying to keep still so my wounds wouldn't rip open when they rubbed against my clothes.

I stayed in my room until four o'clock that afternoon, thoughtless, numb and confused. My father came into my room and told me to take a bath. I couldn't believe after knowing my wounds were open he would make me take a bath. I ran my bath water and got in the tub gingerly.

I felt burning sensations all over my legs, buttocks and on my back. Even on places I didn't even know was injured. I cried quietly and sat stunned. My father's beatings had become one torture after another and even though he saw the physical injuries and the open wounds he had caused, my father showed no sensitivity and it was back to business as usual for him. The lack of love and affection my father showed me stunted me emotionally.

The impact it had on me would be reflected in how I dealt with people from that point forward. My hatred started to go further than just my father.

I knew people had to have heard my cries when my father was beating me, but they chose to ignore them. So I began pointing the blame on others also.

As I sat in the bathtub in excruciating pain, I felt myself hardening mentally and emotionally. I didn't quite know what was transpiring, but I knew something was. I sat there for twenty minutes staring at a blank wall. Thoughtless.

TENNIS ANYONE

My father became interested in playing tennis when I was in the 9th grade and Gerald was in the 11th grade. He would leave early on Saturday mornings and would be gone for hours. When my father took an interest in something, he would heavily invest in it.

He bought several high priced tennis rackets, tennis balls and a cage to pick up the balls. He also bought tennis outfits and several pairs of tennis shoes. He was dedicated to his new hobby and he needed a tennis partner or someone he could play with to help him improve his game. That's where Gerald came in.

My father took my brother Gerald to the tennis courts every Saturday morning at 6:30 a.m. to play with him. Gerald didn't like the idea of going to play tennis with my father, but he knew he had no choice. He had to play well and he also had to pretend to like the game. Gerald came back crying on many occasions. I am not sure what happened, but I just knew he wasn't happy. I assumed it was a typical day with Pops fussing, cursing and even throwing a few tennis rackets at him.

I remember being jealous because my father would take Gerald to play tennis with him and not me. After seeing my brother come home in tears, I was glad my father didn't take me with them.

Gerald told me that my father would yell at him in front of everyone at the tennis courts. He also told me when he made mistakes my father would throw his tennis racket at him.

My father had become so involved with the game of tennis that he started making Gerald get up on school days at 4 a.m. to play an hour or two of tennis. When they got back Gerald had to hurry and take a shower, get dressed and rush to get to school on time.

During one of his P.E. classes, a tennis coach saw Gerald playing tennis with the rest of the kids and asked him if he would like to try out for the tennis team. Gerald didn't like playing for my father, but he did like playing with his classmates at school. He was a little hesitant because of his experience with my father, but he decided to try out for the team since his friends were trying out as well. My brother tried out and instantly made the tennis team. He was really that good. My sport was basketball. I really enjoyed playing whenever I got a chance to. It was a good outlet for me and not to mention I was pretty good.

I often played basketball in gym class, during lunch and during recess. The junior high school I was attending didn't have an indoor gym so the courts were outside. I had become so good that I too was asked to try out for the school's basketball team.

When I asked my father if I could try out for the team, he told me no. No explanation, no rhyme and no reason. Just no. I told the coach my father wouldn't let me try out for the team, but that didn't deter me from playing every chance I could.

I was never allowed to play for the school. No one could understand why my father was against it. Meanwhile, Gerald had been playing exceptionally well on the school tennis team. My father was happy for my brother and thought my brother was good because of him.

I guess teaching my brother the game of tennis made Gerald my father's project, so it was ok for Gerald to play for his school and not me. My brother would go on to win a few trophies at the school.

By this time, my father was really stressing Gerald out over tennis. Every chance my father got he played tennis and dragged Gerald to the tennis courts with him.

Eventually, Gerald didn't want to play tennis anymore. He couldn't tell my father how he felt, but he certainly told his coach at school that he has to quit the team.

Of course, Gerald made sure my father didn't know he quit the team at school. Gerald wanted to tell my father that he didn't want to play tennis with him either, but he knew what the outcome of that would be so he continued to be my father's partner.

My brother would tell me how my father didn't have many friends on the tennis court because of his attitude.

That explains why he chose Gerald to play with him. Unfortunately, Gerald wasn't able to choose for himself.

THE LAST STRAW

I had been beaten almost every day since I've been in the 1st grade. It might not have been as bad had there been some type of love somewhere in there. I've always felt unwanted and a problem child. Everything I did upset my father. Sometimes there was no reason to beat or punish me.

I had dealt with this for quite some time with no changes. I had been very strong and endured so much pain, but there's always a straw that breaks the camel's back. Well, mine came in my 9th grade year of junior high school.

One morning I was getting ready for school and I was about to leave with Gerald. My father told Gerald to go ahead and for me to stay. I was sure it was something I did or didn't do last night, the night before or last week.

It didn't matter to him just as long as he fulfills his desire. Mentally I was already at the point of feeling numb and expecting to be beat and not expecting to be loved. So now it was just my father and I in the house.

My father told me he was whipping me because I didn't put all of the dishes away last night. I told him that I did put them away.

He pointed out that a glass and a saucer were still in the dish rack. I knew I cleaned everything. How did that get there? My father grabbed the extension cord and went wailing away. It didn't hurt as much as it did before. I wondered if it was the tough-skin jeans I had on or that I was numb both emotionally and physically.

Either way I knew I better act as if he was killing me and so the acting began. I hooped and hollered and danced all around the living room. With crocodile tears in my eyes, I told him I was sorry and I wouldn't do it anymore. He stopped and told me to go wipe my face and then get to school.

I wasn't in the best mood for school, but I knew I wanted to be out of the house and away from him. I got my schoolbooks and headed to the front door. I was mad and furious about the whipping. I know those dishes weren't in there last night.

Why would I leave the glass and a saucer? I thought about it and wondered if my mother had used them before she left for work that morning. It didn't matter even if she called and told him she did it he would still find a way to blame me. I walked out the house, down the walkway and to the corner. My father yelled for me to come back into the house. I thought maybe he called my mother and she told him that she left the dishes in the rack this morning.

Maybe he's calling me back to apologize. I walked back inside the house and he was standing at the beginning of the hallway with a mean grimace on his face.

I said, "huh." He told me to come here. I walked closer to where he was standing. I was scared and extremely nervous as always when I was just inches away from him. In a loud, intimidating voice he said, "What the fuck did I tell you about walking out this house without saying goodbye?" I told him that I forgot because I was trying to hurry to school. My father said, "You a got damn lie you're just mad cause I whipped your ass."

Before I could respond to what he said, my father punched me with his fist on the right side of my head. When he punched me, the left side of my head crashed into the corner of the wall and all I was able to see were stars.

I was temporarily stunned. He said some other words that seemed jumbled because I was dazed. When the stars went away, I was able to understand the next set of words that came out of my father's mouth. He said, "Don't you ever leave out this house without saying bye! I don't care what the fuck you're mad at!"

I don't know what came over me, but that was the last straw. I could not take any more of my father's abuse. I dropped my books and took off running towards the front door as fast as I could.

I swung open the front door, ran across the driveway to the side of the house and sprinted full speed towards the backyard.

Not once did I look back. I didn't hear a sound from him, anyone or anything. I got to the tall wooden fence in the backyard and practically hurdled it.

I ran east down the alley to a fenced vacant lot that stored old abandoned cars. I hopped the wired fence, got into one of the abandoned cars and stayed hidden.

I had no idea if my father had seen me hop the fence or not but I wasn't looking to see if he did. About five minutes later I heard a car barreling down the alley. I knew that it was my father looking for me, but I was not going to budge. My heart was racing because I had never done anything like this before. It took a lot of energy out of me.

I didn't know if my father was out there looking for me. So I decided to stay in the abandoned car and lay low for a while. I thought if I stayed hidden long enough my father would think I was far away from the neighborhood. After lying there for about forty minutes listening close for any sound, I fell asleep.

I slept for a couple of hours and when I awoke everything was quiet as I peeked out and looked around. I still didn't see anything so I stayed down. I couldn't believe what I had just done. I actually ran away and it was not planned or even thought out. I wanted to leave many times before, but I never had the nerve. I was afraid of the decision I made but at the same time I felt that I had done something about the abuse.

Others may have looked away, but I could no longer take it. The whole time I was in the car I was nervous, scared and didn't know what my next move would be because I didn't have a plan.

When I finally got out of the car, it was dark and that made me leery of my surroundings. I was on high alert as I looked for my father and his car.

When I saw that the coast was clear I ran until I was out of the area then I began walking. I walked around aimlessly with no direction whatsoever. I was hungry and a little cold even though I had on a jacket.

I walked mostly through the alleys because the alleys were not heavily traveled and I didn't think my father would drive through them looking for me. I remember walking south in an alley that ran parallel to Avalon Blvd. I have no idea why I walked that way, but I knew I had to go somewhere. I saw a liquor store called Smitty's Liquor and I walked in hoping to score by stealing something to eat.

When I walked in, there were two men working behind the counter and a few customers buying things. I grabbed a couple of boxes of Boston Baked Beans and a small pack of cookies. I was going to put them in my pocket, but the man at the counter kept looking at me.

I decided to go to the counter and act like I lost my money. I took my items to the man behind the cash register and pretended to look for my money in all of my pockets.

The man looked me up and down and asked me if I had run away? My jaw dropped as I looked at him wondering how did he know. I didn't know what to say or do. For a second, I wondered if he knew my father.

I was about to run out of the store when he reached into his pocket and handed me a five dollar bill and told me go to the grocery store and get something to eat. I thanked him and immediately left the store. I felt so good because someone I didn't even know cared about me.

My father didn't care one bit when my brother and I were outside all night in the cold with no food or jackets looking for a stupid screw. Who would have thought at 14 years old I would be a runaway? Just the thought of it all brought tears to my eyes and refueled my anger to not look back and keep moving.

I went to the local grocery store called Vons and bought a can of pork and beans and some cookies. On my first night out, I didn't know where else to go but to Enterprise Park by my old elementary school. I remembered the park had a pretty good place I could crash for the night.

My favorite thing to do there was climb to the top of a big eighty-foot robot that had arms you could slide through. The head of the robot was where everyone would go and look out the bars and just yell. After I had bought my items from the store, I made my way to the park through the darkness.

I was scared because I had never been outside in the dark by myself. There were no lights and every sound frightened the mess out of me. I started to walk fast so I could hurry and hide. As I was walking, I was constantly looking around to make sure I wasn't being followed.

I thought the park was a good place to hide and far enough where my father couldn't get me. I was more scared of him than any bad man or bogeyman. When I got to the park, it was completely abandoned. It was quiet and a bit eerie.

I was constantly looking around before I climbed the stairs to the robot. I looked around one more time and then I climbed to the top. When I finally reached the top, there was a very bad stench that reeked of urine. I forgot that was the other thing that kids use to do when they reached the top. The smell definitely took some getting used to but at the same time I didn't care. It was all I had and the safest place for me considering my situation. After all who would look for me here?

So there I was alone, scared, hungry and somewhat cold. I grabbed for my pork and beans and realized I had no can opener. I had no choice but to open my cookies and eat them until I couldn't eat anymore.

I sat in an upright fetal position with my back leaning against the wall. It was getting cold. I took my arms out of my sleeves and pulled the jacket over my head to stay warm.

That actually helped block some of the smell of the urine. That night in the head of the robot seemed like forever to me. I eventually fell asleep and when I woke up I thought I had slept for several hours. I heard the birds chirping which made me think the sun was about to come up.

I learned earlier that birds could start chirping as early as 2:00 a.m. In this case, the birds were chirping but the sun was not even close to coming up.

I slept off and on waking up to weird sounds. It felt wet and cold. The morning did eventually come and I made it through the night. It was my first night away from my family, away from my house and out on my own. I was up at the break of dawn. I didn't know what to do for that day, but I knew I couldn't stay here. Soon kids would be here to play in the robot or walking through the park on their way to school.

I climbed down the robot and began my walk to nowhere. Mentally everything was scrambled.

I had nothing to do and nowhere to go and although I had no plans I still thought it was better than being at home. Since I was hungry I thought going to school would be a place for shelter and food. I tried to go to school as if nothing ever happened. No shower and the same clothes. When I got to school, I made it in time for my first period class. On my way to class luckily, I ran into Tank, who told me my father was in the office looking for me.

Tank didn't know that I had run away the day before so he was just letting me know as we passed each other in the hallway. I had no idea my father would come here looking for me.

I ran out the back of the school as fast as I could. Again, there I was walking with nowhere to go making sure I avoided my father and the police just in case he called and had them looking for me.

FREE TO ROAM

As days went by I stayed in many different places. On some days, I stayed in the pool area at that same park where the robot was located. I slept in the dressing room where they normally change clothes and slept on the cold brick benches. I used the ice-cold bench as my sheet and my jacket as my blanket.

During the day, I searched for different places to sleep because I didn't feel comfortable sleeping in the same place all the time. I found a better place in particular at Athens Park on El Segundo and Broadway. That was more comfortable than the other places I had been so far. There was a baseball field there and behind the home plate area they had a huge 6x6 dugout box where they would keep all their sports equipment locked.

At night when no one was around I broke off the lock, took everything out, closed myself in and that's where I slept.

It was fairly warm inside and I slept better than I did the nights before. Morning came pretty quickly and I was ready to get further away from my father. I decided I would ask my sister if I could stay with her.

I didn't have a way to call her so I had to travel a few miles to get to Compton where she lived.

Before I ran away, Cathy and Tonya had already left home. Tonya lived in Compton and Cathy was living somewhere in Los Angeles. Cedric, my older brother had been out of the service and was living on his own in Compton as well. I had been to Tonya's house in Compton once before with my mother so I knew where she lived.

I began my journey to Compton to see if Tonya would let me live with her. It took me a few days to get there. Along the way, I slept at many different parks as well as junk cars.

I eventually made my way to my sister's apartment on Kay Street right off of Compton Boulevard. When I got there I knocked on the door. Tonya opened the door and I asked her if I could stay there. I told her that I was hungry and needed to eat. She said I could get something to eat but that I couldn't live there.

She told me that my father had threatened her and Rhonda and warned them not to let me stay with them. I said, "Rhonda, is she here too?" She told me that Rhonda had left home too and has an apartment just down stairs.

Wow, I didn't know Rhonda had left home too. I don't know which hurt the worse, my sister telling me I couldn't stay with her or my father having such a cold heart that he would rather see me out in the streets.

Emotionally I was hurt, homeless and alone but I still appreciated any help I could get. I was in no position to turn anything down. I did understand that even though they were no longer in the same household with my father they were still very much afraid of him. We all felt that my father could do anything he wanted to do to us and get away with it.

Thus far, he had gotten away with beating his wife and kids for years undetected.

I was told I could only eat whatever was left and after their kids had eaten. It wasn't much but more than what I had before and I was thankful for that. I hung around the apartment complex and after their kids ate they called me in. After eating, I went back outside because I had to find a place to sleep.

I realized the laundry room in my sister's apartment complex was unlocked. I figured no one was going to do any late washing so I waited around till it got late and went inside around 11 o'clock that night. I made sure I got on top of the dryers. One thing I had learned from my days in what seemed like captivity at home was how to survive. Things seemed to come natural to me. Maybe subconsciously I had learned something from my father after all.

I also learned that I had nothing and no one to turn to. I was away from the house for about two months. I had not showered and I had no change of clothes. I also was barely eating. Eventually, my sister let me in their apartment but only during the daytime.

I had the opportunity to take showers and at night I was back in the laundry room again. I met a few kids around the apartment complex and started playing with them during the day and ate at my sister's house in the evening.

For some reason, I always felt I wasn't getting enough to eat because I was always hungry even after just eating. I guess survival mode kicked in for me because I began stealing from whoever I could even my own family.

Whatever loose change I saw I would pocket it so I could go to the store, ice cream truck or fast food restaurants. Eventually, it wasn't long before they noticed that I was stealing from them.

At that point, they told me that I couldn't come over anymore. I don't blame them because I knew what I was doing was wrong but I was in survival mode and in that mode I could only think about myself.

I began to hang around the kids in the neighborhood more often. At night I was still going to the laundry room in my sisters apartment complex to sleep.

Well that was until one day, the manager told me I had to stay out of the laundry room. So again I was back on the street looking for a safe place to lay my head.

I slept in Lueder's Park that was directly across the street from my sister's apartment. I lived no differently than a typical bum. I slept in nooks and crannies that I deemed safely enough to sleep in.

Sometimes I went without food and other days I got lucky and was able to eat with my friends. One day while I was walking around the neighborhood I ran into my sister Tonya. She told me to call my brother Cedric and ask him if I could stay at his house.

I really didn't want to ask him because I knew he would only fuss at me for running away even though he knew what I was going through at home. I guess my sister felt sorry for me and wanted to suggest ways to help me even though she couldn't help me herself. I didn't call my brother right away because that was something I had to think about.

I loved my brother but he was a grouch and I wasn't yet ready to hear it from him. I continued to stay in the streets near my sister's neighborhood and hang out with my new friends. We would hangout as kids do and although I had nothing, they would let me ride their bikes.

One of the main things we enjoyed doing together was going to the Compton Drive-In. The drive-in was only a few blocks away. We didn't have cars of course, so we would go to the back of the drive-in and climb the 8-foot wall. After we climbed over the wall we would run to the speaker boxes, turn a few of them up high, go back to sit on the wall and watch the movie. A couple of times we were told to get off the walls by security but for the most part we were able to watch a lot of free movies. It didn't seem like much to me, but it took my mind off a lot of my issues.

Well, until it was time to find a place to sleep that night. Some of my friend's mother eventually let me spend some nights, but I don't think anyone knew I was living on the streets.

I was able to take a shower here and there, but my clothes stayed the same. I was wearing the same clothes that I had worn since I ran away. Maybe they did know that I had run away but just didn't say anything. I really enjoyed being around my friends and their families because they treated me well. It was something I definitely didn't receive while living at home. I missed my family a lot don't get me wrong, I thought about Gerald and how much we had been through together.

Of course, I missed my sisters and my mom. I wondered how my mom was coping with me being out on the streets. I wondered if she missed me or if she wanted me to come back home.

It wasn't so bad hanging out with my new friends. The only problem was a guy named Chris. Chris was somewhat of a bully. I had been around bullies basically all of my life such as my father, William and Kurt. So this was nothing new. I didn't know Chris from a hole in the ground and I was not about to be scared of him.

Chris called me out and asked if I wanted to fight. I never spoke to him before and we never had any issues with each other. So I was shocked that out of the blue he wanted to fight me. I asked him why he wanted to fight me and he told me because he didn't like me and he thought I was a punk.

I didn't say anything after that and everyone got quiet and stood around. Then Chris walked up to me and pushed me hard with both hands to the chest. I stumbled backwards. I said, "Quit man, what did I do to you?"

Chris pushed me in the chest again with both hands and again I stumbled backwards. I looked around hoping my friends would break it up because they knew I wasn't looking for trouble, but no one tried to break it up. Chris kept pushing me and then finally the other kids were asking Chris to stop. They told him that we were all just playing and that it was obvious I didn't want to fight.

I got tired of Chris pushing me, but I didn't know how to respond right away. I didn't know whom Chris knew or who would stand up for him and I didn't think I had solid friends to have my back.

I knew I had to do something because Chris was getting a lot braver. So this time when Chris walked up to push me, I planted my feet and swung with my right hand and connected with Chris' jaw. When that happened, Chris grabbed his jaw and started crying. He reached in his pocket and pulled out a fingernail file.

So there we were circling around each other with Chris wielding the fingernail file in front of him. He was still crying, huffing and puffing. He swung at me with the fingernail file and I jumped backwards. He started coming at me wildly and that's when I got stuck with the fingernail file.

Chris had stuck me in the right side of my chest and the fight was over. I fell to the floor and I thought I was dying. Chris took off running and my friends came to me and asked if I was ok. I lifted my shirt and saw the puncture in my chest dripping blood.

My breathing began to labor and I was gasping for air. My friends helped me to my sister Tonya's house and told her what happened. By the time I got there, I was ok, breathing better and barely bleeding. I guess I was overreacting initially because I saw blood, but I was fine.

My sister Tonya put a Band-Aid on the small puncture and that was that. Getting stabbed in the chest scared the crap out of me. I no longer felt comfortable being out there in the streets. I also knew Chris and I would end up fighting again and Chris doesn't fight fair. I decided to go with my sister's advice and ask my brother Cedric if I could live with him.

Cedric was living in Compton on Alondra Boulevard at the time with his wife Denise. They didn't have any children and they both worked for the Post Office. Cedric agreed to let me stay with them but not without him scolding me for running away.

He thought I should go back home because I was too young to be living on the streets. I knew he was right, but I told him I wasn't going back home.

I couldn't believe that after all the abuse he'd experienced with my father he would suggest that I go back.

That was the last thing I wanted to hear. I needed someone to have compassion for my situation. Of all people, I thought he would understand. Cedric was very strict and use to living alone. I was not planned, so it was a little strain on him with a new wife and all. He didn't care about the threat my father put out there for those who helped me.

After the showdown Cedric had with my dad, Cedric was no longer afraid of him and my dad knew it.

Cedric commenced to put down the rules. He told me that I had to get back in school, I couldn't stay out late and he didn't want me to run in and out of his house. I already didn't like all these rules, but I didn't like sleeping in the streets either so I agreed.

Cedric bought me a few clothes and a pair of shoes. I finally felt human. As if I belonged to someone. He made sure I had enough money to catch the bus to school and back. I eventually went back to school at Vanguard and although I was very nervous about my father showing up there he never did. I finished the remainder of the school year and graduated from the 9th grade. I didn't exactly walk the stage because of my grades, but I did get promoted to the 10th grade.

I was still at Cedric's house and was able to hang out with my friends because Cedric was at work most of the time. One day I didn't have any money to eat and wanted to have some change in my pocket. Cedric had a huge jar of change in his room and I began stealing a few quarters at a time for candy.

Before I knew it, I was stealing dollars. One evening, Cedric noticed a lot of the money in the jar was missing and went looking for me. He drove to my sister's house and they brought him to where I normally played with my friends.

He was furious when he saw me. He made me get in the car and they took me to the Compton Police Station. While there, he told the policeman at the desk about my situation and he wanted them to take me to Juvenile Hall.

The policeman said they couldn't do anything with me. Cedric got mad and told the policeman that I had stolen money from him and my two sisters. I looked at my brother and thought to myself, "I didn't steal any money from Rhonda." I guess he was pouring it on thick to make it sound bad.

The policeman told him he was sorry but they couldn't keep me. I guess my brother just wanted me off the streets for my own sake but at the time I didn't like how he was trying to do it. Again the policeman told him he was sorry, but that there was nothing that could be done without my parent's permission since I was under age. I was free to go and this didn't sit well with Cedric.

He didn't know what else to do so we left the police station. Cedric was still angry and told me I could no longer stay with him.

Again I was back in the streets. I was on my own and no longer welcomed in my older siblings house. Of course, that was my own doing.

My siblings helped me as much as they could, but I was getting out of hand. I eventually started hanging around my other friend that lived closer to our house. He lived close to Vanguard Junior High School. His name was Calvin. Calvin was a mild mannered kid that didn't pick on anyone but when you crossed him you had a major problem on your hands.

We got along good at school because we both loved the game of basketball. Calvin had two brothers older than him and one younger. The two oldest were your neighborhood tough guys. They weren't your normal bullies, but they weren't the type that would stop a fight either. When I was hanging out at Calvin's house, his older brothers were not around much. Neither was his younger brother.

Calvin and I played basketball a lot and afterwards we would go to his house and eat. I am not sure if I told Calvin I was out on the streets or if he just assumed I was, but he knew. Calvin asked his mom if it was ok if I could spend the night with them from time to time and she approved. I spent every night I could at their house. I spent the night around 3 times a week there and I ate there almost every day.

When I didn't spend the night over Calvin's house, I spent the night at Athens or Enterprise Park.

I had lived at Calvin's house off and on for about a month before I made him my next victim. I noticed there was a coin bank in his mother's room.

Initially, I tried to resist it but eventually the temptation got the best of me. I stole a few quarters from his mom's coin bank when no one was in her room. I don't know what got into me. Calvin was super cool with me and his mom was so thoughtful to even allow a stranger into her house. It started with me taking small amounts then it escalated until much more.

I knew I had to leave. I was disappointed in myself yet at the same time I did what I did. I've heard and read many stories about thieves and I was becoming one.

The same day I stole the money I left and didn't come back. I knew that once Calvin's mother found out that someone has been stealing her money, Calvin and his two older brothers would be looking for me. I couldn't blame them and had the shoe been on the other foot I would do the same.

I practically ran out of places to go. I have burned so many bridges with my survivor mode attitude. Not only was I homeless but also I was on the run. I ended up going back to a place I was very familiar with. Enterprise Park. I hung around the park during the day and mostly I played basketball outside to kill time.

At night, I quietly climbed the tall robot where I would sleep until the early morning. I was glad it was summertime for many reasons. One reason was that free lunches were given to all the kids at the park and I made sure to get two lunches by telling them one was for my brother.

The other reason was that it wasn't as cold at night. I spent a lot of time to myself and thought more than I used to think when I was in my room at home. I thought of the bad things that were done to me and how life was at that moment.

I didn't feel good about myself at all. I didn't see anything promising. There seemed to be no hope.

A few days passed and I was sitting in the park passing time trying to make it through another day. I was sitting on a bench in front of the swimming pool when suddenly I turned around and Calvin and his two older brothers were right behind me. I have no idea how they found me, but they did.

I heard one of his brother's say, "So you want to steal from my mama huh?" Before I could run Calvin's two brothers began hitting me while Calvin watched. Actually, I'm not sure if he watched or if he was getting his licks in too. I was too busy trying to cover up. When I got a chance I got up and ran as fast as I could.

I did not look behind me. The punches didn't bother me because I felt I deserved it and brushed it off. Needless to say, I never stepped a foot in that park again.

I really was starting to miss my mom, sisters and brother even more. I was tired of being alone and in the streets going nowhere and living dangerously. I started to compare my life as it was today and how it was before I ran away. I wondered if running away was such a good idea after all.

Regrets were setting in fast. Part of me was thinking maybe I shouldn't have run away and the other part of me reminded me that I hadn't received any beatings in months. As soon as I thought about my father's beatings, his verbal abuse and the way he abused my family, I felt my actions were warranted.

In the entire 8 months I was gone, not once did I miss my father. In fact, every thought of him angered me. I did my best to keep him out of my mind. I hoped my mom and siblings were doing ok. I wondered if Gerald was still playing tennis every morning via shotgun. I wanted so bad to go home, but I didn't want to be there as long as my father was home.

It felt like my body was still healing from all the beatings I had received. Whenever I had the opportunity to shower, I would notice all the scars that my father engraved in my skin.

Reminders of why I had to leave. I may have been healing physically but mentally my psychological healing would take more time.

SOUTHERN COMFORT

With nowhere to go and no one else to turn to I decided to ask my grandmother if I could live with her. It was my mother's mom and I knew my dad would not go there.

It took a lot for me to ask her because I didn't want my mothers side of the family to know what was going on. I felt so embarrassed. I was a prideful person and very private and if I went there I knew everyone would know.

My mom's side of the family was more upscale. You didn't hear about incidents such as mine happening on her side of the family. There was already small talk going on about our family because of my father and I didn't want to add to it.

Unfortunately, I had no choice in the matter and I had to swallow my pride. My grandmother didn't live too far from Athens Park where I was sleeping some nights.

In spite of me wanting to protect my privacy, I'm sure that side of my mother's family already knew that I had run away.

My grandmother was a sweet, loving, warm and soft-spoken woman. I don't think she could scream if she tried.

She was about 66 years old and she was in great health and spirit. My mom looked a lot like my grandmother and had a lot of her mannerisms. My grandmother had a light brown complexion. She was medium build with straight gray hair.

She easily resembled a native Indian. She often smiled and when she did her eyes would get tight and her cheeks would rise to the occasion. Always looking happy and peaceful. Big Mama was what we affectionately called her. She would not turn anyone down if they needed a place to stay.

When I called her, she told me I could stay with her as long as I agreed to go to school and clean up around the house. This was the type of woman she was. Open arms and open heart. I was still nervous about going there. Not because of my grandmother but because of my pride.

I finally made it to 122nd street where Big Mama lived. The neighborhood was quiet with perfectly manicured lawns and stylish homes. The houses there didn't have front gates. That made it more uniformed and neat. Everything looked open and peaceful.

As I was walking down the street, I stopped in front of Big Mamas house, took a deep breath and walked in the front door.

Big Mamas house was never locked. Everyone knew just to walk right in. When I walked in Big Mama was right there sitting on her laminated couch. I said, "Hi Big Mama". She had a huge smile on her face that lit up the room.

She said, "Hello Michael". I loved the way she pronounced my name. It was very southern and welcoming. She got up and gave me a hug. It felt so good to be in the arms of a loving parent even though it wasn't my immediate parent.

Big Mama had a nice modest house. It was full of love and the air was filled with peace. It had two bedrooms, two baths with a den and a living room. Just outside of the house to the back was a garage where she said I'd be sleeping. My cousin Phillip and my uncle Nate were also living in the garage.

Big Mama called Phillip into the house and told him I would be staying in the garage with them. Phillip was the same age and the same height as I was. He was dark skinned and was quiet and more like the nerdy type without the glasses. He had a pretty good head on his shoulders. He wasn't bad or wild he was very mature for his age.

We weren't the best of cousins and we never hung out with each other prior to me coming there. He and his mom had visited our house every now and then, but he never really wanted to hangout much. His mother Sonia was cool with my dad so she was the one that visited my mom a lot. Phillip had been staying in the garage for a while. I'm not exactly sure how he got here, but he seemed happy where he was. He walked me to the garage and showed me the top bunk bed where I would be sleeping. The garage was converted into two rooms with a divider in the center. Phillip and I shared the back room and my uncle Nate had the front room.

It wasn't your typical garage. The walls were paneled and the floor was carpeted. It was actually quite cozy but most importantly peaceful.

Uncle Nate and Phillip both were introverts. They kept to themselves and were both even tempered. Uncle Nate always seemed to have a smile on his face just like my grandmother. He didn't talk much at all.

Uncle Nate and Phillip were always on the go. Phillip was around his friends in the neighborhood most of the time and Uncle Nate was out in the streets doing whatever he does. There wasn't too much to do at Big Mama's house. I didn't have any friends and I wasn't trying to meet any.

I was doing what I was accustomed to doing, floating with no plan. I really didn't have anyone to reach out to and I didn't think my grandmother would understand me.

Either that or I didn't want to burden her with more than what I had so far. So I tried to figure things out for myself. I'm sure news had gotten back to my mother and father that I was living with my grandmother.

As crazy as my father was, I knew he wouldn't dare show out in front of my mom's side of the family and demand I leave my grandmother's house. He was crazy, but he wasn't stupid. Well then again maybe he was both. He was able to control my mom and his kids, but that was as far as his controlling went.

Besides, he didn't want anyone to actually see how mean and cruel he really was to us. Both of my parent's family knew that my father was mean to us, but they never saw him in his true form. He was great at putting up a front whenever he was around them.

After being there a few days, my father had sent some of my clothes to my grandmother's house, which was a surprise because no one asked him to do so.

I think it was just a cover up to make himself look good or he just wanted to make a statement to me. Maybe it was his way of saying that he was glad I was gone.

Staying at my grandmother's house was wonderful because I was at peace and I finally had a roof over my head. The most important part was that I was living with family and not strangers. Although I appreciate my friends and their families that welcomed me into their homes, it was nothing like being around your family.

Different members of the family came over all throughout the day and the environment was wonderful. My grandmother always showed me love.

She made sure I was comfortable and doing okay. It was something I wasn't used to, but I didn't mind getting use to it at all. At my grandmother's house, I slept like a baby. I slept for 12 hours almost every night. I woke up one morning and my grandfather was in the yard cleaning up. I offered to help him and he pointed out a few things for me to do.

He knew I was now living there, but he didn't ask me any questions. I guess some things are best kept unsaid. My grandfather was sterner than my grandmother yet he talked to me with respect.

Although he was stern, he was genuinely a loving man. One of my fondest memories of my grandfather was when he used to come to our house on 130th St. every Friday.

He would get off work and bring each of us a box of Cracker Jacks. He never came inside our house. Instead, he would park in front of the house, get out, get his hugs and give us our cracker jacks and leave.

Just by looking at my grandfather you would think he was a mean old man. He had a menacing look like he was always frowning. But my grandfather was the most loving husband, father and grandfather you could ever have.

My grandparents were a great couple and had been married for over 50 years. My grandfather was average height with a light brown complexion.

His hair was balding in the middle and he kept it short. He didn't take any mess and would tell you how he felt, but he was never rude or disrespectful in doing so.

My grandparents complimented each other very well and were a couple to emulate. My grandmother enjoyed cooking and would cook all the time. Throughout the day, some of her kids and grandkids would come through just to sit around, eat and talk.

She enjoyed everyone's company and seemed to be content just to take care of her family. It was your typical Big Mama's house where everyone felt comfortable just being himself or herself.

A typical day at big mama's house for me was helping out around the house doing whatever my grandfather asked me to do or watching T.V. in the garage until it was time to go to sleep.

HOME SWEET HOME

I had lived at my grandmother's house for a couple of months now and during that time I hadn't seen or heard from my mother. I assumed my father wouldn't allow her to come see or call me. I just wished that one day I would get to see my family soon.

A few weeks had passed and my wish was answered. I got some news from my aunt that was hard to believe. She told me to call my mother right away because my father was no longer living at the house. The news definitely took me by surprise.

I was told that something happened at the house that forced my mother's hand. This incident made my mother tell my father he had to leave. I was shocked of the news. I wanted so bad to know the extent of the situation. What could have happened to make my mother finally stand up to my father?

I only imagined it had to be something inhuman. The things that had been going on in that house for years would have been enough for the police to be involved a long time ago. I could only imagine the happiness of Gerald, Diane and Sharon that my father was gone.

I imagined it must have been similar to getting the news that President Abraham Lincoln freed the slaves. That's how happy I felt that day. I felt free. I felt redemption. I felt relieved but at the same time I was concerned because the news seemed surreal.

Doubt came over me and my excitement began to calm. Maybe my father would find his way back to start the terror all over again. Maybe he would find a way to convince my mom to allow him back in the house. After all, mentally he had controlled her for so long. I had to double check to make sure that the news was true.

I got on the phone to call my mom so that I could ask her myself. When I called, the phone rang once and I hung up because I was scared. What if the information was wrong? What if he answered the phone? I didn't even want him to know that it was me on the other end.

I thought about it and asked myself what could he do to me? I was in a safe place and he couldn't do any more harm. I got up enough nerve and called again and this time I let it ring until my mother answered the phone. She said, "Hello". I said, "Hi mom this is Michael". She said, "Hi Michael, did you hear that your father was gone?" I said, "Yes I did and that is why I was calling. I wanted to hear it for myself".

She confirmed that my father was gone and told me I could come home. I asked her if he was coming back and she told me that he was gone for good.

There was some silence as I held the phone and then the tears began to roll down my cheeks. It's been so long since I heard my mother's voice and to hear her say come home was music to my ears. I thought finally my father was no longer going to torture any of us again.

I tried to fight back my emotions, but I couldn't. To think that all the abuse we had suffered as a family was finally over gave me a heavy heart. I had a lot of questions, but I decided I would ask her when the time was right.

I told my mother I would be coming home in a couple of days. We hung up the phone and I stood in my grandmother's kitchen smiling, still crying but smiling.

My grandmother asked me what was wrong? I told her that my father was no longer in the house and that my mother said I could come home. She said, "I know, I heard, isn't that great news?"

I told her yes it was and then I thanked her for allowing me to stay there and I told her I would be leaving in a couple of days.

She told me that I was welcomed and she told me to get my life together.

I went into the garage and wanted to tell anyone that was in there, but I was alone. I yelled, "Yessss", real loud. I was elated and in disbelief at the same time.

I had taken a crazy chance to run away from home at a young age only to be happy to return.

I had so many questions and thoughts. I wondered how my siblings that were still at home felt.

I wanted desperately to ask them what happened and I wished I had been there to see it for myself. I was anxious about going home, part of me wanted to go home and the other part of me wasn't ready.

I have been gone since I was 14 years old and now that I am 16 a lot has changed. I know it doesn't seem too long, but time on the streets seems like forever. I couldn't explain it, but I was torn and had to sleep on it to make sure it wasn't a dream. I had to make sure that my father wasn't coming back and what I'd heard was real.

Two days went by and nothing had changed. My father was still gone and it was finally time to go home.

I woke up that morning a nervous wreck. I did a lot of thinking while lying in bed and at the same time I was building up my nerve. It was around 12 o'clock noon when I decided to pack my belongings. I didn't have much to pack as everything I had fit into a shopping bag with room for more. I said goodbye to Big Mama and thanked her again. I got into Uncle Nate's car and off we went.

It was a quick drive to our house and before I knew it we were there. I wished we'd lived just a little further so I could compose myself. As we got to our street, I noticed it was different. At least it felt that way because I had been gone for so long. My uncle Nate dropped me off in front of the house. I thanked him and told him goodbye.

He drove away but somehow I wish he'd stay just long enough for me to get in the house.

I was nervous and I was having second thoughts but I was here now and there was no turning back. There were no signs of my father's car. It was just my mom's car parked on the street in front of the house. I walked up the driveway and to the front door. I had not seen my mother and siblings for a while and now I'm finally home.

Nervously, I rang the doorbell and my heart started racing. I couldn't say it was because of one thing because I wasn't sure of anything at that moment. As I was standing there I peeked through the bar door to the garage. Thoughts went through my head of the horrible ordeals that happened in there. I quickly shook those thoughts from my mind.

I wanted to come with a clear mind and I had to fight any negative thoughts. I heard someone trying to open the door and when it opened I saw my mother. I was instantly relieved.

We said, "Hello" and hugged. It felt a little awkward, but I guess this wasn't a normal situation. I walked inside the house and closed the door. She told me she was cooking so she briskly hurried into the kitchen. She said, "Your room is still your room so you can go put your things away".

I walked around the living room looking at everything I could as if I never been there before. I was looking to see if things had changed or if it was still the same.

Even though I had been gone a long time I noticed some changes. The furniture was in different positions than it used to be and some other things had been moved around as well.

Even though my father wasn't there, somehow I could still hear the screams, the yelling, the beatings and the crying. The fear was still heavy in the air as if it was fresh.

I could see that scared little boy in me trying not to be seen, not to be heard and not to be beat. Emotions welled up inside of me all over again, but I hid it well as I always had. In fact, my siblings and I had a way with masking our emotions so that no one would know how we truly felt. We hid our emotions from my father and my mother. We hid it from my mother because we didn't want her to feel any worse than she already did.

I walked to the beginning of the long hallway of death and just stood there. For some reason, it wasn't as long as I originally imagined. Maybe it was because I have been gone, or that the hallway seemed long because I was either walking to my doom or for my safety. I began walking down the hallway. As I passed by each room, I peeped in to see if anyone was in there.

When I got to my room, I stopped and pushed open the door. When the door swung open there was no one inside.

The room looked the same with two twin beds on each side of the room. My bed didn't have any linen on it and looked as if it hadn't been slept in.

I wasn't ready to go inside just yet. I also didn't want to feel trapped. Standing in the hallway allowed me to know if someone came through the front door. I always thought my father had a personal vendetta against me and that he took my running away as a personal challenge. A challenge he hadn't had a chance to settle.

From the doorway memories started flashing before my eyes. I saw that little child getting beat over and over as "The Monster" was swinging the extension cord faster and faster. I heard the screams and the cries. It felt like yesterday.

I didn't realize my breathing was a little erratic. I began to hyperventilate from all the thoughts that were running through my head. I tossed my bag onto my bed from the doorway and walked away from the room.

After being calm for so long and away from my father's abuse I realized that I was still on edge and the painful memories were fresher than I thought. No one else was home besides my mom and I. She was cooking and we didn't say much to each other. I had a lot of questions, but I knew right now was not the best time to ask them. I think my siblings were either at the store or out with their friends enjoying the freedom that we never had before.

Being at the house definitely had me on pins and needles but it was something I knew I could get over. Gerald and Sharon had finally come home. The only person that didn't was Diane. Gerald told me that when my father left he took Diane along with him.

I knew Diane didn't want to go with him, but I am certain she had very little choice in the matter. Just when I thought all of my siblings were finally safe one was still in harms way. This news put a damper on my spirits. Talking to Gerald and Sharon, I could tell they were much more relaxed than ever before.

They were happy and very talkative. Our emotions were always subdued and even though my father wasn't there we were programmed, emotionless replicas of him. We never showed that we cared for or loved each other but deep down we knew we did even though it was unspoken.

After the food was ready my mother told me to fix my plate and eat. Usually my mom would fix everyone's plate and set it on the table. This was totally different.

I went inside the kitchen and made my plate. I felt like a guest in the house when I should have felt at home. Mom had cooked fried chicken, mash potatoes and peas. Gerald and Sharon made their plates too, but they were in the living room eating and watching T.V.

Now this was new to me because we were never allowed to eat in the living room. I definitely saw some major changes that would take some getting used to. I sat at the dinner table. I didn't yet feel comfortable eating in the living room or with Sharon and Gerald. After eating, we all watched T.V. with my mom.

We didn't talk much and my mother and I had yet to really talk about anything.

I am not sure if she was embarrassed by what happened to me all these years or if she was personally going through things herself.

Later that night it was time to go to sleep. It was about 11:00 p.m. that night. I was sleepy from all the anxiety I had been feeling about coming home. My mother had put linen on my bed. I made up my bed, turned the lights off and lay down. Gerald was still in the living room watching T.V. I was lying on my back looking up into the darkness thinking about all that transpired to where I am now. I couldn't help but cry as I lay there. The thoughts of my beatings ran like a film in my head.

Earlier I had looked at the shell of a mother I had. He took a lot from my mother and he took a lot from me. It was all just too sad and I wished I could just sleep so I wouldn't think about all the living nightmares. Somehow I finally dozed off. Throughout the night, I would toss and turn and sleep on and off. Literally every sound startled me. I finally fell asleep in the wee hours. I heard a loud sound that woke me up out of my sleep.

It was the sound of the bedroom door being kicked in and the light being switched on. I jumped up and it was my father with the extension cord wrapped tightly around his hand. He was sweating profusely and breathing rapidly. In his other hand was a whiskey bottle. He appeared to have been drinking straight from the bottle and it was almost empty. He said, "Get your ass up!" I was scared to death. My heart was pounding and I wanted to scream.

Before I could open my mouth, Gerald shook me to wake me up and told me I was making noises in my sleep.

My heart was pounding and it didn't seem like I was sleep at all. I never had a nightmare before so this was new to me. I told Gerald thanks for waking me and that I was having a nightmare. Gerald went back to his bed and went to sleep. I lay there, sleepless, with the covers over my head until morning.

As the days went by I was able to relax more and sleep better. I continued to have an occasional nightmare, but they became far and few in-between.

As time went on it seemed like everything was back to normal. My mother didn't micromanage us like my father did. She did yell a lot, but that was usually after she'd come home from drinking with her family. I didn't like that she was drinking, but I knew it was because of what she had gone through with my father. If drinking helped fight the demons in her head, who am I to judge her.

At this point, we all have demons we have to deal with, especially me. I wish there were something to help me fight the demons I was facing as well. How and when I was going to deal with mine was going to be my next challenge. I am not sure if I was prepared for this challenge, but something inside of me has always pushed me along.

ABOUT THE AUTHOR

Mike Antheny was born and raised in Los Angeles, California where he currently resides. He is the seventh of eight children. He has always been considered the more creative child in the family. He started taking pictures at a very early age in which it ultimately became not only his passion, but also his profession. Writing was something Mike Antheny knew he would eventually do because of a burning desire to share his own story.

Five years ago, during the time of writing this story, Mike realized that writing became therapeutic and helped him deal with what was deep inside and therefor he thought just maybe it could help someone else. With that in mind Mike Antheny's passion for writing grew even larger as he began writing more thought provoking books.

Follow Mike Antheny www.mikeantheny.com/Facebook/Twitter

CarPerTina Books

www.ingramcontent.com/pod-product-compliance
Lightning Source LLC
Chambersburg PA
CBHW061430040426
42450CB00007B/982